THE
WINE & BEER
MAKER'S
YEAR

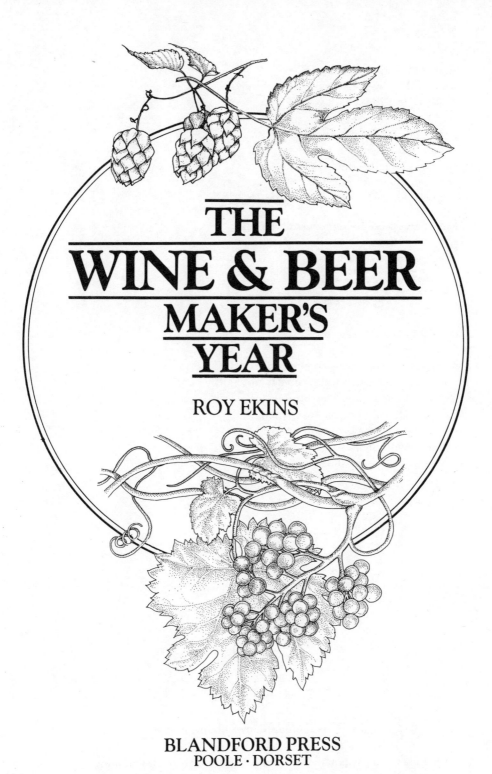

THE
WINE & BEER
MAKER'S
YEAR

ROY EKINS

BLANDFORD PRESS
POOLE · DORSET

First published in the UK 1985 by
Blandford Press, Link House, West Street,
Poole, Dorset BH15 1LL.

Copyright © 1985 Blandford Press Ltd

Distributed in the United States by
Sterling Publishing Co., Inc.,
2 Park Avenue, New York, N.Y. 10016

British Library Cataloguing in Publication Data

Ekins, R.
  The wine and beer maker's year.
  1. Wine and beer making—Amateurs' manuals
  2. Brewing—Amateurs' manuals
  I. Title
  641.8'72   TP548.2

ISBN 0 7137 1541 3 A

Typeset by Megaron Typesetting, Bournemouth, England

Printed in Great Britain by Butler and Tanner, Frome and London

CONTENTS

ACKNOWLEDGEMENTS

Acknowledgement is due to:

Cyril Berry, until recently Editor of the *Amateur Winemaker* and its associated series of books on our hobby, and to his successor, Argus Specialist Publications Ltd, for all the knowledge gained over the past twenty years from those publications.

Professor G. Fowles, for permission to use material from *Must*, and information absorbed in recent years from his other publications.

Vanessa Luff, whose delightful illustrations have added so much to this book.

All those associated with our hobby who have in any way added to the experience that has led to this book being compiled, and whose names are too many to list.

My thanks to you all,

Roy Ekins
Formby, 1985

With love to Irene, my wife, and Vivienne,
Paul, Stephanie and Jeremy, who
all bore with me patiently.

AN INTRODUCTION TO WINEMAKING AND BREWING

Yeast is a small and simple fungus that derives its energy from sugar. It leaves behind it two main by-products, carbon dioxide gas and ethyl alcohol. And there, in a nutshell, is the underlying basis of the whole huge world of alcoholic drinks. All through that vast range, from low alcohol table wines and beers to fierce high alcohol spirits, such as whisky, rum and brandy, the process of production depends at some stage on this microscopic plant's brief but busy life.

Let us look at these alcoholic drinks in turn. Wine, in the world of commerce, is usually defined in terms such as 'the product of the fermentation of freshly expressed grape juice'. From this, the inference is clear: drinks made by fermenting the fresh juice of crushed grapes are wine, drinks made by the fermentation of other ingredients are not. If that were generally accepted, then home-winemakers would have to find another description for their delightful drinks. But so also would those manufacturers – dare we call them vintners? – who import concentrated grape juice, dilute it, ferment it with yeast, and sell it labelled as 'British Wine'. There are also many other wines commercially produced abroad from other sources, including palm wine, or toddy, from the sap of the palm tree, the various fruit wines made from soft fruits and berries in most European countries and the Japanese spirit, sake, which is distilled from a form of rice wine.

Even a tightly defined description of wine, however, cannot become universally acceptable, or even be enforceable, except perhaps in the labelling of goods for sale, because of the many anomalies in the commercial trade itself. Apart from those already mentioned, there are obvious examples, such as port wine which after only a few days of fermentation is virtually sterilised by a massive addition of grape spirit. The many aperitifs and vermouths available all started as grape-juice wines, but have subsequently been adulterated, and usually improved, by the addition of herbs, spices, peels, juices, bitter flavourings and other modifying ingredients. Many also have spirit added to strengthen them beyond the alcohol levels reached by fermentation.

So clearly we can discount this restrictive view of what constitutes a wine and, instead of regarding only fresh grape-juice wines as being deserving of that title, we should use those wines as setting the style and the standards for our wines from varied ingredients and model our recipes to simulate the acid, sugar and tannin levels found in grape juice so that the wine yeasts we employ are provided with the living conditions that best suit them. Thus we will ensure that the yeasts will give

1

the best results and supply us with eminently drinkable beverages, well balanced and with attractive bouquets, that deserve the honourable title of wine.

Winemaking in the United Kingdom was, until the 1950s, very much regarded as a cottager's occupation and either mocked as a practice where dear old ladies made highly explosive bottles of appalling fluids from unmentionable substances, or regarded with awe as something one's grandmother did with rhubarb and elderberries and baker's yeast, producing powerful elixirs that would stun a hardened drinker after just one wineglassful. Undoubtedly there is an element of truth in both these beliefs. Unskilled winemakers can produce some revolting liquids. True, homemade wines often contain 14% or more alcohol compared with the 8% to 12% of ordinary table wines, and two or three glassfuls on an empty stomach will certainly have some intoxicating effects.

But, generally speaking, the homemade wines of our forbears were lower in alcohol content than those of today and frequently contained ginger or other strong spices to mask the off-flavours arising from faulty techniques and unsuitable yeasts. Following the huge growth in our hobby in the last 30 years or so, winemakers in the United Kingdom now have access to a variety of pure wine yeasts, a great range of ingredients, easily available specialised equipment and modern techniques and materials that practically guarantee good drinkable everyday wines, with superb wines occasionally that will be long remembered and appreciated.

With this great upsurge in the numbers of winemakers came a continuing growth in the number of societies devoted to furthering their members' knowledge of commercial wines and making wines at home. Frequently these are known as 'Wine Circles', a circle being looked on as the best description of a group of friends with similar interests and ambitions. Wine Circles are immensely popular and, as well as advancing the knowledge and skills of their members through lectures, tastings and competitions, also have as a rule a lively social side, organising outings, dances and other functions, such as dinners and barbecues. Membership of such a local society is strongly recommended, if only for the specialised knowledge and friendly help that is immediately available, though anyone who does join a Circle is almost certain to join in at least some of the activities. Your local homebrew shop will probably be able to put you in touch with the Secretary of the nearest Circle.

With the formation of the early Wine Circles, C.J.J. Berry of Andover published a small newsletter and recipe sheet, which rapidly grew into the monthly magazine *Amateur Winemaker*. This caters for all lovers of the homebrew hobby and is the magazine that reliably reflects the current news and reports of new products, major shows and Circle newsletters, as well as articles by recognised experts in their fields and items of general interest and amusement. Another more recent arrival in the field is *Practical Winemaking and Brewing*, which, too, has a growing circulation and reputation.

Major competitive shows and conferences are run by Federations of Wine Societies throughout the country each year and, in addition, there is an annual national show run by the National Association of Wine and Beermakers. These and other competitions are judged by the National Guild of Wine and Beer Judges and by accredited judges of the various regional Federations. All these judges have qualified by examination of their knowledge of winemaking or beermaking and by a practical test of their skill as judges, after they have proved their ability by gaining awards in open competitions.

Amateur beer-brewers, a term used to cover those who make beers, ales, lagers, stouts, barley wines or any other beverage produced by fermenting malted grains or extracts of them, have the same support from the homebrew trade and from the Circles, Federations, National Association and guilds of judges previously mentioned. All these bodies relate to the hobby as a whole. What is special about homebrewing is that, in this instance, the amateur is fermenting his drinks from the same ingredients as the professional brewer. There are, of course, some exceptions – you can't often buy a commercial nettle or spruce beer – but in the vast majority of cases, beers, stouts and lagers are made from a malted barley grain, or extract, with hops in some form, and fermented by one of a very few types of yeast. The ingredients available to the homebrewer may not always be of the same high quality available to the brewers, whose huge purchasing power can guarantee them the top of the market, but the tremendous growth in homebrewing has brought with it a noticeable improvement in the marketing and the quality of the materials available to the amateur.

Until 1963, in the United Kingdom, it was necessary to have a private brewer's licence to make beer at home, subject to various Excise restrictions. No such restriction has ever applied to winemaking at home. In the Budget that year, the Chancellor, Reginald Maudling, gained for himself a permanent niche in the history of homebrewers by abolishing all restrictions and licensing requirements except one: beers made at home, like homemade wines, may not be sold or otherwise used to raise funds.

This naturally gave a tremendous boost to the hobby and many new kits of grains, malt extract syrups and powders, with hops or hop concentrate flavourings, have appeared on the market since. The amateur brewer now has a great range of kits available, as well as a large choice of ingredients for the brewer who likes to produce better beers by the same methods of mashing, boiling etc. used by the professionals. In consequence, the homebrewed beers and lagers found in competitions today are far superior to those of 20 or 30 years ago.

William Cobbett's *Cottage Economy* of 1822 encouraged the making of beer at home from cheap and wholesome materials, with a consequent saving of money. Although modern commercial beers are wholesome enough, the difference in cost between commercial and homebrewed beers is quite marked. Cobbett's remarks, now terribly dated in their attitude, still hold good over a century and a half later, though I feel, that homebrewed small beer is unlikely to replace the tea he so despised.

The third and final type of drink referred to is spirits. The Alcoholic Liquor Duties Act 1979 strictly prohibits the manufacture of spirits by distillation of a fermented liquor or by any other process in the United Kingdom by any person, unless he holds an Excise licence for that purpose. The penalties are severe, including fines of £1000 and confiscation of equipment, materials and fermented musts. If you link this with the dangers inherent in distillation without expert knowledge, there is no doubt that the gamble is simply not worth undertaking. Apart from the legal punishments, there is a possibility of the dabblers in distillation producing spirits that are actually harmful to their health and that of their friends. Methyl alcohol is lethal; tragically, hardly a year passes without deaths being reported following a party where it has been used to spike a bowl of punch. Yet methyl alcohol boils at 148.5°F (64.7°C) compared with 173°F (78.3°C) for the drinkable ethyl alcohol, so any methyl alcohol in a wine will be separated by distillation before the ethyl alcohol is volatilised. It is unavoidable and it can kill.

Incidentally, it is possible to remove some of the water content of wine by freezing it and straining out the flakes of ice. This is regarded by the Customs and Excise as manufacture 'by any other process' and it is as illegal as any other method of making spirits at home.

So home production of spirits cannot be considered. However, by careful infusion of fruit, herbs etc. in alcohol, or blending commercial spirits with sugar syrup, flavourings and homemade wine, it is quite easy to produce liqueurs of pleasing flavour and satisfactory strength at a fraction of the cost of their commercial equivalents.

To summarise, wine can be freely made, as it always has been. Beers can now be made at home without licence. Spirits cannot be made at home, but can be blended with homemade wine using spirits on which excise duty has been paid.

Now let us go on, to learn how these delightful drinks can easily be produced, to give pleasure in their making and enjoyment in their drinking.

WINEMAKING : BASIC PRINCIPLES

Before we actually launch into the whys and wherefores of making wine, it is as well to know clearly just what it is we are setting out to do. Commercial wines are incredibly varied, from dainty light white and rosé table wines through to heavy sweet ports and Madeiras, yet remarkably few of the recipes published for making wine at home give the novice any indication of the sort of wine to expect when it is finished. All too often one hears comments like 'Oh, apples, they do make a strong wine, don't they?' And so they can, but they will make light low alcohol table wines, dry sherry-style wines and heavy rich dessert wines as well. In most instances, the type of wine you produce should be decided before you start to make it, not just by how it turns out at the end. Can you imagine the chaos that would ensue if vineyard owners couldn't predict what kind of wine their grapes would ferment into year by year?

Let us look at a light white table wine, say a Mosel from Germany. This comes in a tall slim bottle, green to protect the wine from the daylight which would discolour it, and with a label that complies in detail with the strict German wine laws. The wine itself will have a fresh flowery bouquet from the Riesling grape and a crisp flavour with a good tangy bite from the high malic acid content. The alcohol content is fairly low, usually around 9%.

Compare this with a sweet red wine, such as a port. Even a comparatively inexpensive ruby port will be full-bodied, very sweet, high in acid – though the sweetness masks it – and strong in alcohol. Although a ruby port is only aged for 2 or 3 years before blending and bottling, it has a depth of character, a complexity of bouquet and flavour that an ordinary Mosel would never have. The two wines are as different as can be, and it is this variation that must be borne in mind if you are to make the most of the ingredients you grow, pick wild, or buy for making into wine.

To emulate the elegance of a Mosel calls for pure and delicate ingredients, with perhaps flower petals to enhance the bouquet, and care taken to preserve the pale colour throughout the winemaking process. A wine like port needs to be heavy in fruit, tannin and acid and fermented with lots of sugar so there is a residual sweetness as well as a high alcohol content. The fruit needs to produce a stable colour of great depth. Damsons give a good bouquet and low colour; blackberries have a wonderful flavour but a colour that turns to tawny brown; elderberries have a great depth of beautiful red pigment, lots of tannin, but a flavour that needs a little mellowness adding if long maturation is to be avoided. So there we have three popular and easily obtained fruits, none of them really suitable alone. But just try blending them and that way you will find that you can get all the attributes you need to make a wine of great character and colour, equal to any but the most expensive port.

Some adjustment is essential in almost all wines made from ingredients other than grapes, to produce a well-balanced must for fermentation. Even grapes can need some adjustment; the commercial vintners occasionally need to 'chaptalise', or add sugar, to the juice of their grapes in years when the weather has prevented the crop from ripening satisfactorily. And, of course, the majority of wines on sale are blends of two or more wines, to standardise the product of that particular supplier or that certain type of wine. Grape juice is still as near a perfect material for wine as there is. Homemade wines from other ingredients invariably and understandably need some adjustments before the must can have the yeast added. Fruits vary in their sugar and acid content, depending on the weather, where they have grown, how ripe they are, what the juice content is and what particular varieties they are. Flavour is similarly affected, and so are tannins, pectin and a host of other variables. Flowers contribute little but colour and fragrance; grains generally give a wine a slightly harsh spiritous flavour. Root vegetables vary tremendously; green vegetables are almost all unsuitable.

These are only generalisations, but without doubt there is one golden rule that always holds true: the best quality ingredients make the best wine. Occasionally someone will produce a superb wine from, say, bruised or mildewed oranges, or labour lovingly for months to produce a wine from onions or radish-tops or some other outlandish ingredient that takes 5 years to become drinkable. Of course these remarkable events happen – the world is full of strange happenings, like showers of frogs and hailstones like tennis balls – but it must be accepted that they are abnormal. As one pundit stated, such wines are a triumph of technique over ingredient. So by all means, have a bit of fun and try a celery-and-runner-bean sherry if you wish to, but don't rely on such ingredients to provide you with a regular supply of good drinkable wines. Especially if you want to keep your friends!

Let us now progress to learn more about winemaking. Notes on all the various ingredients will accompany the recipes given later in this book, but here are a few notes of general application.

Ingredients
FRUIT

When you buy soft fruit in bulk, it comes in shallow trays or baskets, so that the weight of the fruit does not bruise or damage the lower layers. Bear this in mind when you gather fruit from your own garden or allotment, or from the hedgerows and bramble patches. Squashed or bruised fruit will make wine, of course, but it tends to deteriorate in quality very quickly. It is also susceptible to damage by moulds and mildews and will quickly be infected by the bacteria that produce acetic acid, the active ingredient of vinegar that makes wine undrinkable. Be warned, wine vinegar is very nice for kitchen use, but a gallon goes an awfully long way.

If fruit is bruised or damaged, be ruthless and cut generously to remove any spoilt parts. Over-ripe fruit has already started to decay by the destructive action of the fruit's own enzymes and such fruit is generally to be avoided.

With dried fruit, one can reckon, in practice, to use a quarter of the amount one would use of fresh fruit. Dried fruits almost always benefit from scalding with very hot water and then soaking for a few minutes. This is because a variety of chemicals is used to preserve and bleach the fruit; oils or glycerine are sprayed on some to keep them soft and pliable. Alas, some bacteria have learned to adapt and survive these various processes and will multiply in your wine, possibly spoiling it, if you do not sterilise the fruit beforehand.

Fruit is also available in tins and the quality is usually high, with no waste. Tinned fruits also keep without further care until they are required for use. It is often possible to buy cans of fruits that are not readily available fresh, such as paw-paw, mango and lychee, or have only a short season, like blackcurrants and strawberries.

Deep-frozen fruit, whether purchased or of your own freezing, quickly breaks down when thawed. Because of this the fruit is more easily crushed and the juice flows more freely than with fresh fruit. Another advantage is that the pectin content, which can cause hazy wines, is reduced by storage under freezing conditions. Deep-frozen fruit keeps for months and is a useful source of winemaking materials in the winter.

Many fruits are readily available as fruit pulps and concentrates. Fruit juices too are now easily purchased and come in great variety. Some of the blended juices include exotic tropical fruits and are well worth trying out as the basis for a wine. One of the 1-litre (just under 2 pints) packs of juice now on sale is sufficient to make a gallon (4.5 litres) of wine. These are available all the year round.

FLOWERS

Flowers are delightful if freshly picked. Never store fresh flowers or petals in a plastic bag or box; they will rapidly decay, become smelly and slimy and quite unfit for use. They can be deep-frozen from fresh without loss of quality.

Dried flowers are obtainable from herbalists and homebrew shops and should be used in small quantities; an ounce or two (30 – 60g) is usually enough to replace the quart or so (1 litre or more) of fresh flowers most recipes call for.

Both fresh and dried flowers are useful to the winemaker, to enhance the bouquet of what would otherwise be a dull wine to one's nose. Such flower additions must be made extremely sparingly. Rosepetals and elderflowers are most commonly used for this purpose. Do, however, beware of one quite common error: an elderflower bouquet does not suit an elderberry wine.

HERBS AND SPICES

These are not used so much nowadays as they used to be, though enthusiats keep turning out the odd batch of rosemary, lemon thyme, mint and similar wines from garden herbs. Of them all, the best is probably parsley, which makes a wine with a clean fresh flavour and an attractive but very faint pale green colour.

Spices are more often used for flavouring a wine made primarily from another ingredient. Root ginger is probably the most popular and gives a wine a touch of fieriness that makes it seem stronger than it is and successfully masks any slight faults in the flavour.

Generally speaking, herbs and spices are nowadays being used more and more by winemakers who blend their own to try and match the elusive flavours of commercial vermouths and other aperitifs – and liqueurs. This is a fascinating field in which there is an endless range of variations and mixtures that could quite easily amuse a home winemaker for the rest of his or her life. And there is always the possibility of evolving a new flavour that will be a commercial success, though it is indeed a remote chance.

GRAINS

There are not a great many popular wine recipes that include grains, e.g. rice, wheat, barley, though grain in some form is the basic material of all the drinks in the great family of beers. If you make wine with grain in it you will find it helps to soak the grain in a vacuum flask of hot water for a few hours. After the water has been drained away, the grain is more easily crushed or coarsely minced.

Grains sold in grocers, health-food or homebrew shops may appear expensive compared with those from other sources, but in your own interests it is advisable not to buy your maize or wheat from a pet-shop or animal-feed chandler. The pet-foods may be cheaper, but the grains may be infected with weevils or beetle larvae or contaminated with mouse or rat droppings that may well carry bacterial sources of disease. Freshly harvested grain from the farm is of course perfectly acceptable.

STORAGE

Canned and bottled fruits and juices will keep perfectly for many months, preferably under cool dry conditions. Heat may lead to deterioration of the contents and moisture will quickly form pinholes in tinplate through rusting, allowing bacteria to contaminate the contents. Blown or leaking tins should always be discarded as a potential source of poisoning.

Fresh fruits, such as apples and pears, will keep for some time on wooden racking in a cool dry atmosphere. Make sure that only perfect unblemished fruit is used and inspect it regularly. Remove any specimens showing signs of decay, as any rot will quickly spread to the surrounding fruit.

The simplest and probably most effective way of preserving fruit is by freezing. Small quantities of berries will freeze quite satisfactorily in a plastic freezer bag or a box with a clip-on lid and are ready for winemaking or even, if you have a surplus, for kitchen use. Only perfect fruit should be used for freezing. Larger quantities, such as apples by the sack, can be frozen for 48 hours or so, and then allowed to thaw in a plastic bucket or bin. Once thawed, the fruit can be crushed easily or pressed to extract the juice. If the juice is not to be used straight away, it can be refrozen until required. Emply plastic ice-cream boxes are ideal for this as their tapered and flexible sides make it easy to remove the blocks of frozen juice. These can be wrapped in individual plastic bags and stacked in one corner of the freezer, out of the way. Using this method greatly reduces the volume taken up by the fruit, leaving room for other domestic foods to be stored. Or even more fruit!

Dried foods are mostly prepacked nowadays, but if you do buy loose dried fruits, store them in an airtight container until required. Herbs, if fresh, can be dried in a very slow oven, with the door left open, or simply hung upside down in bundles in a cool airy place, such as from a garage or attic roof. Once thoroughly dried, they should be roughly crumbled and stored in airtight containers. Screwtop jars that have contained instant coffee are eminently suitable and look quite neat when appropriately labelled.

SUGAR

Although the grape produces sufficient sugar to make wine in most years, few other fruits do. Most of the fruits native to the United Kingdom have such a high acid content that the juice has to be diluted with water and sugar has then to be added. Diluted juices do not contain sufficient sugar to make a wine with enough alcohol in to preserve it, and sugar must be introduced. Sugar is a blanket description for a variety of materials, such as sucrose, fructose, glucose and maltose. Ordinary domestic granulated sugar is sucrose and it is immaterial whether it is derived from cane or beet. Sucrose comes in many forms, such as icing and caster sugar, brown, Demerara and Muscovado. There is nothing to be gained from using icing or caster sugar and they are more expensive than granulated. The various brown sugars are supposedly healthier for you than the white sugars, but yeasts don't seem to care. Using brown sugars will affect the bouquet, the flavour and the colour of your wine and should not be used without taking these factors into account. Brown sugars can be used as part of the formulation for some rich sweet dessert wines such as malmsey and sweet brown sherry, but otherwise are best excluded. Preserving sugar gives no advantage, nor do the prettily coloured decorative coffee sugars, but again, they cost more than granulated.

You will come across old recipes occasionally that refer to candy or loaf sugar. Pure white sugar used to be crystallised into cones weighing around 10 – 15 lb, (4.6 – 6.9 kg) and was broken up or cut up for table use. Modern techniques of production are incredibly more efficient, and candy sugar has been succeeded by 2¼ lb (1 kg) bags of granulated sugar. Another antique still occasionally referred to is 'foot sugar' – the sugar crystallised in the bottoms of barrels of molasses and raw sugar imported for the sugar refineries.

Of the various syrupy materials available, all give wine a distinctive flavour. Molasses, treacle and golden syrup are all fermentable, but the residual smell and taste of these ingredients are usually unmistakable. Corn syrup and wheat and barley syrups are occasionally available through homebrew sources or baker's suppliers and can be fermented. They too tend to modify the flavour of the wine slightly.

When the yeast feeds on the granulated sugar as a sucrose solution, it does so by producing an enzyme, sucrase, which reduces the sucrose to two simpler sugars, fructose and glucose. This process is known as 'inversion' and can be brought about by the winemaker boiling his sugar with water and a teaspoonful (5g) of citric acid, but as this acid has to be taken into account in formulating the recipe, and the 'invert' sugar only shortens the fermentation by a day or so, it really isn't worth the bother.

Invert sugar can be bought, but again it is more expensive than granulated. It comes in sticky blocks and one and a quarter times as much as ordinary sugar has to be used because of its water content.

Fructose is usually on sale, often labelled as 'fruit sugar'. There is no need to incur the extra expense; this also applies to glucose. Glucose can be bought as a fine white powder or, a little more cheaply, as coarse lumps of pale brown material looking like fudge and known as 'glucose chips'.

Granulated sugar, therefore, supplies almost all the needs of the winemaker. It is most efficiently used by boiling 2¼ lb (1 kg) of sugar in approximately 1¹⁄₁₀ pints (625 ml) of water. One pint (560 ml) of this solution equals 1 lb (450 g) of sugar, ½ pint (280 ml) equals 8 oz (225 g) and so on. Using sugar in the form of sugar syrup makes it much easier to mix it in with the other ingredients, reduces the need for a lot of stirring to get it dissolved and blended in the bucket or fermenting jar, and avoids the wasteful and irritating foaming that occurs when sugar grains are added to a fermenting must. If you wish to see this effect, sprinkle half a teaspoonful (2.5 g) of sugar into half a glass of fizzy lemonade; now imagine the mess caused by adding 8 oz (225 g) of sugar to a gallon (4.5 litres) of fermenting red wine must. As soon as your sugar syrup has boiled it will turn perfectly clear and it should then be removed from the heat, covered and left to cool ready for use. Any surplus can be stored in an airtight bottle for use in the next few days.

There is one other form of readily obtainable sugar not yet mentioned: honey. Honey is mainly used for making mead and other honey-based drinks. These are cyser (honey and apple juice), pyment (honey and grape juice), hippocras (honey and fruit juice) and metheglin (honey and herbs). All these are fermented with yeast in the usual way. Honey is also used as an ingredient in wines where another ingredient is dominant, in which case it simply replaces part of the sugar. The addition of honey will alter the bouquet and taste of a wine, as fermented honey has quite a distinct aroma and flavour of its own. This natural invert sugar is not sterile and must be dissolved in warm water and gently raised to simmering point, when a scum of wax, pollen etc. will form and should be skimmed off. The honey and water solution should then be allowed to cool and used without delay. Honey should never be boiled, as this drives off the fragrance derived from the flowers which the nectar came from. Different honeys produce slightly varied wines and meads.

ACIDS

From 3.5 to 6 parts per thousand of acid, measured as tartaric acid, need to be present in wine for it to ferment well, the variation depending on whether the wine is light or heavy-bodied and whether it is to be drunk as a dry or a sweet wine. Heavier, or thicker, wines contain dissolved materials, including sugar and some non-fermentable substances that act as a 'buffer' to the acidity of the wine, reducing its impact on the tongue and palate. Light dry wines taste more acidic as there is less to affect the palate than in a heavier sweeter wine.

The main acid of ripe grapes is tartaric acid and this acid does not predominate in any other common winemaking fruit. It is, however, a useful acid for the winemaker as, if by mischance, the wine is more acid than you wish it to be, sudden chilling will result in some of the excess acid precipitating as cream of tartar crystals (potassium tartrate) or with time it will occur naturally. These crystals are known as 'argols' and are occasionally noticeable in the bottom of bottles of white table wine.

Unripe grapes contain malic acid and this is the principal acid in apples, rhubarb, most of the stone fruits, such as cherries, plums and damsons, and also in pears. Malic acid is subject to attack by a particular species of bacteria which reduces the acid to the milder flavoured lactic acid, and leaves the wine, if bottled, pleasantly sparkling when its cork is drawn. This is easily avoided by good sterilisation practice when the wine is bottled.

Citric acid is the traditional acid used by winemakers, probably because, in years long past, oranges and lemons were the only readily available source of acid suitable for use; other fruits high in citric acid are strawberries, blackcurrants and raspberries. Citric acid is now easily obtained in pure crystalline form, but is produced from molasses by another type of fermentation.

Malic and tartaric acid are also available in crystalline or powder form.

Many fruits, such as plums and oranges, and all their relatives, are sufficiently high in acid, even after dilution, not to need any additional acid. However, recipes based on low-acid materials, such as banana or carrot, need 1 – 2 teaspoonfuls (5 – 10 g) of acid adding, as do wines based on flowers.

Oxalic acid, found in minute quantities in a few fruits, is the poisonous acid found in the green leaf of rhubarb and this part of rhubarb must never be used. The amount available elsewhere is very small and can safely be ignored.

Succinic acid is produced as part of the development of wine during maturation and is believed to assist in providing the eventual bouquet of the wine. The addition of succinic acid to a wine must does not seem to have any appreciable effect.

Finally, to the acid already mentioned earlier that spells disaster to the winemaker. Acetic acid is the main constituent of vinegar and once vinegar can be smelled in a wine it is irretrievably ruined. Acetification is brought about by bacterial infection and careful and hygienic techniques of winemaking should prevent its occurrence. The infamous 'vinegar fly' (*Drosophila melanogaster*) is the ordinary fruit fly and this carries the bacteria to the fruit or the fermenting must. Cleanliness and care are the only preventives that are needed to defy its approaches.

Measuring the acid content of a must is a relatively simple process and instructions are given in Appendix 1. In broad terms, a must from acid-free ingredients needs 1½ – 2 teaspoonsful (7.5 – 10 g) of acid, whereas one from low acid ingredients needs about 1 teaspoonful (5 g) per gallon (4.5 litres). High-acid fruits, like oranges, plums and blackcurrants, need no additional acid at all. Many old recipes specify the juice of an orange and a grapefruit, or of two lemons, to provide the acid in a wine must. You need only look at your greengrocer's shelves to realise the absurdity of this; acid content depends on the size of the fruit, the quantity of juice it contains and its degree of ripeness. Surprisingly, the riper a lemon is, the more acid it contains. One or two recipes in this book do specify the use of citrus fruits in order to enhance the flavour of the main ingredient and, in such cases, good juicy fruit of top quality, and the size specified, should be used.

Excess acid can be reduced by adding 1 level teaspoonful (5 g) of calcium carbonate (precipitated chalk) or bicarbonate of soda, which will counteract 1 part per thousand of acid, with some foaming from the carbon dioxide gas released. Don't use more than 3 teaspoonsful (15 g) or the flavour may be affected. To increase acidity, 1 level teaspoonful (5 g) of tartaric acid will add roughly 1 part per thousand of acidity.

TANNINS

Tannins are essential, in red wines particularly, and in all but the lightest white wines. Without tannins, wine is soft and flabby, lacking bite, zest and a lot of character. Tea is high in tannin and young wines with excessive tannin will shrivel the gums and fur the teeth just like a well-stewed cup of tea. The skins of apples and pears, red fruits (such as blackberries, elderberries and blackcurrants) and various oddments, such as oak leaves, come high in tannin and should not be left fermenting for too long, or be used in too high quantities unless the wine is to be matured literally for years.

Red grape skins contain tannin, which is why many red wines need to be stored for a long time for the slow chemistry of maturation to combine some of the tannin and the acid and to leave a mellow wine with great depth of flavour and bouquet. Without a high tannin content, the wine could not last so long in a healthy condition.

Excess tannin can be reduced by fining the wine with gelatine, but it is usually preferable to blend the wine with one of a low tannin content, store the wine to let time reduce it naturally, or even to mask it by adding a little glycerine to the wine. This should be done in stages, by trial and error, as the glycerine will also slightly sweeten the wine.

WATER

It may seem odd to discuss water, but let's face it, it is the major ingredient in homemade wines. Tapwater from a domestic supply is usually suitable for winemaking. It is not sterile, but is near enough so for the risk of introducing an infection or wild yeast into the must to be negligible. Water that is very hard can be boiled and allowed to cool to remove some of the hardness, which forms a sediment, but may need re-aerating by pouring it backwards and forwards from one bucket to another, to ensure suitable conditions for the yeast. Distilled water should not be used as it is quite free of all the dissolved mineral salts which the yeast needs for growth.

YEAST

Four thousand years ago a Theban king was buried in Egypt and all the trappings of royalty and supplies for the afterlife were interred with him. Modern analysis has identified one of the clay jars as a beer jar. In the scraping of sediment in the bottom of the jar was a yeast which proved to be *Saccharomyces winlockii*. The ancient Egyptians made half-baked cakes of grain and the same yeast has also been found in them.

This is the earliest example of yeast used for fermentation, though there is evidence that wild yeasts were among the earliest living plants on Earth, traced back at least to the Devonian ages, over 300 million years ago.

The first recorded wine was that of Noah, from whom traditionally sprang the first post-Deluge agriculture and, particularly, the cultivation of the vine. There is an old story that God gave Noah the vine to make wine because the waters of the Flood tasted of sinners, but the truth probably lies nearer to the fact that the grape vine *(Vitis vinifera)* is native to Asia Minor where Biblical events are believed to have taken place. Where there are grapes, there will be yeast and doubtless, at some stage, a pot of grapes or grape juice would have fermented and been tasted out of curiosity. For centuries this blessed fluid poured from the vineyards of the shores of the Mediterranean – millions of gallons of wine. Strangely, not until 1857 was it proved by Louis Pasteur that yeast was the cause of fermentation. Previously scientists had believed that fermentation and decay alike were spontaneous happenings and any micro-organisms found were considered to be merely associated with putrefaction, or even to have arisen from it. Pasteur demonstrated that a living organism had to be introduced into any sterile medium to cause change; living yeast was shown to be essential for the start of the fermentation process.

From this innovation followed the ability to produce pure cultures of selected strains of yeast. Natural yeast sources, such as the bloom on grapes, also include many other organisms that are not wanted by the winemaker, such as the spores of moulds and mildews, bacteria and wild yeasts that give the wine off-flavours, or even reduce the precious alcohol to water. Being able to sulphur the crushed grapes, which stuns or destroys the wild strains, and to inoculate them with a pure culture of the chosen yeast brought about a revolution in commercial wine production, giving a reliability and a degree of standardisation and continuity not previously known.

Apart from one or two experimental vineyards, the United Kingdom had been without a native wine-growing industry since Roman times. Despite this, winemaking continued, but only at domestic kitchen level. In consequence, winemakers had to resort to unsuitable yeasts for their winemaking. The most easily available were the barm used for leavening bread dough and the brewer's yeast, which are in fact the same thing, *S. cerevisiae*.

Happily for the hobbyist, pure wine yeast cultures started to appear on the United Kingdom retail market in the 1950s, and the quality of homemade wines has improved tremendously in the succeeding decades. Because appropriate yeasts, mostly strains of *S. ellipsoideus*, are now being used, winemaking has also become easier and the end product more reliable and predictable. Wine yeasts are normally slightly sticky and form a cohesive sediment which does not rise easily when the wine is racked or poured. Clearing the wine is thus easier and, as a higher alcohol tolerance is inherent in wine yeasts, there is far less danger of ending up with a syrupy low alcohol fruit juice, full of unfermented sugar. The introduction of wine yeasts to the amateur market was probably the biggest forward step in the hobby in centuries.

Yeast, being just a simple little fungus – insofar as any living creature can be called simple – asks for little from life. Provide it with a suitable medium to live in, preferably a sweet, slightly acid liquid with minute amounts of mineral nutrients dissolved in it, and the yeast is happy. It proves this by multiplying at an incredible rate – by a primitive sexual method, by splitting in half, and by growing lumps, known as buds, that form new adults. A remarkably versatile plant, the yeast wants nothing more than to feed to provide energy for reproduction. A small liquid culture of yeast can, within 2 or 3 days, change a gallon of wine must into a seething fermentation containing something like a million million living yeast cells. As a rough comparison, that's over two hundred times the entire human population of the world.

The yeast continues to feed, to multiply and to die until the alcohol content of the must reaches the yeast's tolerance level or, if the alcohol level is not attained, until the whole of the fermentable sugar present has been consumed. The yeast then slowly sinks to the bottom of the container, forming a fairly firm deposit, leaving above it a limpid wine. The approaching end of a fermentation is often visually marked by the top inch or so of the must falling clear; it is then only a matter of time until the whole of the wine is clear. At that stage, it is advisable to rack the wine off the sediment, i.e. to remove the clear wine by means of a syphon tube.

Cheap yeasts are often selected strains of bread yeast and are not recommended. Yeasts sold by the drum are also of dubious value as they quickly deteriorate once opened and are also prone to contamination by airborne spores of other micro-organisms. Wine yeasts are usually retailed in small quantities, either sealed in foil and plastic sachets, as powders or tablets of dried yeast, or as sealed miniature bottles of a liquid culture. Any of these added to a gallon (4.5 litres) of must should ferment satisfactorily, activity such as clouding being obvious within about 48 hours at 70°F (21°C). For larger quantities of must, or to be certain of a quick start to the fermentation, a 'starter bottle' can be used. This is simply a sterilised bottle, in which is placed ½ pint (280 ml) of a cool solution of boiled fruit juice and water, with 3 teaspoonsful (15 g) of sugar dissolved in it. The yeast culture is added and the container sealed with a hand-pressed wad of cotton wool or a scrap of polythene sheet held in place by an elastic band. Of course, if the container will take an airlock, this is to be preferred. Keep the starter bottle at 70 – 75°F (21 – 24°C) and the yeast growth will quickly cloud the liquid. Within 1 or 2 days, it will be fermenting, with tiny gas bubbles rising in the container and becoming visible at the edge of the meniscus (where the surface rises slightly against the side of the container). As soon as this occurs, the contents of the starter bottle can be used and a quick start to the bulk fermentation is certain.

A small amount of the starter can be kept back, further sterile solution added and the container recapped. The yeast will again multiply rapidly and can be used to start another fermentation or can be kept in a refrigerator, still sealed, until required. It is then only necessary to add a little more sugar and to allow the temperature to rise in order to reactivate the culture; it can even be shaken up and simply added to the awaiting must.

In theory, as long as perfect sterile procedures are carried out, it should be possible to reproduce a wine yeast this way indefinitely. In practice, due to its fantastic rate of reproduction, some mutated cells will eventually survive and multiply and the purity of the culture will be lost. As it is, in any case, almost impossible for the amateur to maintain sterile conditions, it is advisable to use a yeast only two or three times before replacing it. This will avoid many difficulties in determining just why a wine is substandard in clarity, flavour or bouquet.

Whatever you do, ignore recipes that include such archaic ideas as floating the yeast on a slice of toast, leaving the must to be fermented by an airborne wild yeast, or even (yes, it's true) adding a piece of twig from a hawthorn hedge to save using yeast. This last gem clearly shows that folklore hasn't advanced much since pre-Pasteur days. A piece of twig carries only wild yeasts, usually the very last thing you want to introduce into your valuable wine must.

NUTRIENTS

Yeasts are microscopic specks of plant life; those that feed on sugar are named *Saccharomyces*, which simply means 'sugar fungus'. As small plants, they need just the same foodstuff that larger plants do. Obviously organic manures and mulches that you would put on your rosebed or onion patch are not the sort of thing you would like in solution as a drink, so instead we provide the yeast with chemical fertilisers. A level teaspoonful (4 g) of ammonium phosphate to the gallon (4.5 litres) provides the yeast with nitrogen and phosphorus, and most of the other trace elements are dissolved from the main ingredients. Occasionally a slow fermentation can be livened up with a ¼ teaspoonful (1.5 g) of Epsom salts, which provides magnesium. This level of the salts will not have a laxative effect on the wine-drinker!

Besides the mineral salts there is one organic substance that can assist fermentation. Yeast produces, and seems to enjoy the presence of, Vitamin B compounds. These are destroyed by the sulphur dioxide which winemakers use as a sterilising agent, so it often helps to add one crushed 3 mg Vitamin B compound tablet per gallon (4.5 litres).

Winemaking Process

EQUIPMENT

This can be as complicated as you want, or as expensive as your purse will let you indulge, but complex and expensive equipment is not necessary for you to produce wines you will be proud of.

Take winemaking at its simplest; making wine from a tin of concentrate off a shop shelf. Let's be honest, that's how most winemakers start, and many never make wine any other way. Kit wines have improved so much in recent years that excellent grape wines can be made with little difficulty.

For a basic wine like these you will need: a tin-opener, a funnel, a demijohn (1 gallon/4.5 litres fermenting jar), a bored rubber bung, an airlock and a syphon tube. Additionally you will want a teaspoon and a larger spoon for stirring, and a large pan or kettle for boiling water. The tin-opener is standard and the funnel is a simple plastic funnel so that the liquids can be poured into the demijohn through its narrow neck. The demijohn is best made of glass with a small neck. Those sold for winemaking hold slightly over a gallon, so that a full gallon (4.5 litres) of finished wine can be syphoned off the yeast deposit. Demijohns may be of clear white or brown glass, the latter being slightly more difficult to use but having the advantage of protecting the wine from the daylight that might otherwise spoil its colour. Demijohns are said to get their name from a corruption of *Dame Jeanne*, a French

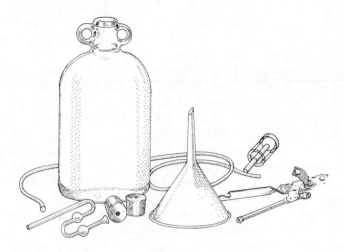

name for oversize bottles generally, that are used for *vin ordinaire*. Cider and some other liquids are sold in glass demijohns that hold just 1 gallon (4.5 litres) and these are perfectly satisfactory for winemaking. The plastic gallon containers at present on the market are porous to gases and a variety of ills to plague your wine can come from their use – odours from nearby onions, jars of paint-thinners, disinfectants, fly sprays, perfumes, soaps – anything that is near the container or has been inside it. It is almost impossible to remove the taint left by the previous contents of a secondhand plastic container, and even new ones can flavour your wines with the fillers and solvents used in their manufacture.

While the must is fermenting, it is susceptible to various infections and must be sealed off from the open air. The fermentation produces carbon dioxide gas which must be allowed to escape from the jar. This dual purpose of protection and gas release is quite simply effected by the use of an airlock – a simple water trap. This is fitted into a bored rubber bung and the bung is pushed into the neck of the demijohn. The airlock is then half-filled with water and the dust-cap fitted to exclude flies and their friends. This arrangement protects the wine and, as gas is produced, it pushes out past the airlock, giving rise to a characteristic plopping noise. Bored corks are not recommended for this purpose, as they often have large internal cracks and are notoriously unreliable.

The syphon tube is usually of clear flexible plastic tubing, about 5 ft (1.5 m) in length. This is used to transfer liquids from container to container, to avoid the splashing that takes up oxygen and may spoil a light wine. The commonest reasons for such a transfer are to remove wine from any sediment it is standing on, a practice known as 'racking', and to run finished wine into bottles for storage.

Spoons for measuring small amounts of nutrients and for stirring are normal kitchen equipment, as are the pans and kettle that are occasionally required. At this level of winemaking, nothing else is needed until the wine is bottled, when you will require corks or stoppers and bottles to put the wine in. Remember, a gallon is 8 pints but only six bottles of wine. A helpful gadget which makes the job much easier is a corking machine of some sort.

This equipment is sufficient to make any wine made solely from juices or syrups. As soon as solid ingredients, even flimsy things like flower petals, are included in the recipe one has to consider how the juice, the flavour, the bouquet, or whatever else the ingredient supplies can best be extracted. Usually, fruit is crushed or pulped and fermented for a short while in a bucket, and then strained through a cloth into the demijohn. Buckets should be new, nylon or white plastic for preference, and kept only for winemaking. Nothing is worse than to spend months turning those precious hand-picked blackberries into a wine that tastes finally of wallpaper paste or detergent from a misused bucket. Don't even use your precious wine buckets for beermaking if you can avoid it, as a few stray beer yeast cells can quickly multiply in a wine must, giving a very disappointing end result.

Straining is done through a muslin, terylene or nylon net bag, or a colander or similar strainer can be lined with a fine cloth. For larger quantities, I use the plastic soil riddles sold for garden use, and lay a piece of terylene net across the top of it. If you have no suitable piece of equipment, a piece of cloth laid loosely over a bucket and fastened in place with half a dozen spring clothes-pegs will work perfectly well. When the straining is complete and you are removing the cloth full of discarded pulp, take care that none of it slips back into the bucket.

Steam and electric juice extractors, wine presses, fruit crushers, all have their place in winemaking. These you will acquire as your expertise grows and your enthusiasm expands with it. Don't be tempted to go out and spend a lot of money on equipment initially. The list at the start of this section, plus a couple of buckets and straining cloths, will be sufficient for a gallon of most wines, and odds and ends, such as zesters, which remove only the coloured part of the peel of citrus fruits, and capsulers, which neatly apply coloured foil capsules over the cork and the neck of a bottle of wine, can be bought as and when the need arises. You will of course need an extra demijohn, bung and airlock for each gallon (4.5 litres) made, until your first wine is finished and bottled.

The range of equipment is so great that every pocket can be catered for; when birthday and Christmas presents are being considered, a carefully-dropped hint can work wonders!

HYDROMETERS AND SPECIFIC GRAVITY

A hydrometer, or saccharometer as a purist might say, is a simple device that gives an approximate measure of the amount of sugar in solution in a must or wine. The more sugar there is, the higher the specific gravity (SG) of the liquid compared against a reading of 1.000 for water at 59°F (15°C) at sea level. The more sugar there is, the denser the liquid and the less deeply the hydrometer sinks into the must. The deeper it sinks, the lower the specific gravity reading on the scale on the hydrometer and the less sugar in the solution.

Because of the surface tension of the must, the wine rises slightly at the edges where it meets the side of the test jar and the stem of the hydrometer; this curving

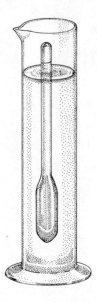

surface is known as the meniscus. For greater accuracy the reading should be taken looking from slightly below surface level, rather than from above.

As the fermentation progresses, so the yeast uses up the sugar, and this is reflected in a continually reducing specific gravity reading. When the fermentation ends, the specific gravity can easily drop below 1.000 if all the sugar has been used up, as alcohol has a lower SG than water and the wine is of course a mixture of the two.

A hydrometer can be very useful in checking the original gravity before fermentation starts, and at stages later. This allows you to measure the amount of sugar in your ingredients before you add any other sugar and to check the progress of the fermentation. From hydrometer readings you can find the sugar content at any time and can calculate the probable or potential alcohol content of the wine when it is finished from the total amount of sugar consumed, i.e. the initial quantity less what is left at the end.

However, it must be pointed out that the readings from a hydrometer are only approximations. Variations of more than a few degrees of temperature will make a significant difference to the readings, as will an undue amount of fruit pulp, no matter how finely divided, in the test sample. Lastly, a fermenting must or a young wine has a quantity of carbon dioxide gas in solution in it. This must be driven off by shaking the sample in a bottle or stirring it well in the test jar with a glass rod or a sterilised knitting needle.

A table of specific gravities, sugar content and potential alcohol is included in Appendix 2 and can be read simply across to determine whichever figure you require. For example, an original specific gravity of 1.090 shows that the full gallon (4.5 litres) contains 2 lb 7 oz (about 1.1 kg) of sugar and has an alcohol potential of

14½% by volume. In theory, the alcohol content should be slightly higher, but in practice the full potential is never attained and this is recognised in the table.

As a general guide, 1 gallon (4.5 litres) of must containing 2¼ lb (1 kg) of sugar should have a specific gravity of 1.085, and produce about 13½% alcohol. This is quite sufficient strength for a red table wine. Each additional 4 oz (115 g) of sugar adds about 0.01 to the specific gravity and nearly 1½% to the potential alcohol.

As a practical example, let us imagine we are making a light table wine, using 4 pints (2.3 litres) of apple juice and 8 oz (225 g) of sultanas. For this wine we want about 10% alcohol, so aim for an original (starting) gravity of 1.065. This represents total fermentable sugars of 1 lb 12 oz (790 g) in the gallon (4.5 litres).

The apple juice has a specific gravity of (say) 1.045 so there would be 1 lb 4 oz (565 g) of sugar in a gallon (4.5 litres) of juice. As we have only half this quantity of juice, it contains just 10 oz (285 g) of fruit sugars. Sultanas and other dried grapes average a sugar content of 10 oz per lb (285 g per 450 g) so our 8 oz (225 g) will contain 5 oz (140 g) of sugar. We now have a little sum, thus:

Total fermentable sugars needed	1 lb 12 oz (790 g)
Less:	
Sugar in apple juice 10 oz (285 g) ⎱	
Sugar in sultanas 5 oz (140 g) ⎰	15 oz (425 g)
Domestic granulated sugar to be added	13 oz (365 g)

This will ferment out to below 1.000 SG and may need sweetening very slightly to be palatable.

STERILISATION

We do not aim, as winemakers, to provide sterile conditions comparable to an operating theatre in a hospital. Absolute sterility is not our target and, generally speaking, little more is wanted than the usual level of hygiene found in a well-kept modern kitchen. We are though, dealing with living organic ingredients, living yeasts to do the work, and far longer periods of time in which stray yeasts or bacteria can wreak havoc than is normal in other types of kitchen activity. A few wild yeast cells won't ruin a trifle or a fruit tart because it is consumed long before they can have any effect, but bacteria will spoil many foods within a short period, and unpasteurised milk will curdle within a few days. And everyone knows that cheese or bread will quickly grow a blue-green mould if left unrefrigerated.

Clearly, then, even the clean kitchen has its own population of microscopic life and, because winemaking is usually a process lasting months, or even years before the last bottle of a brew is drunk, extra steps have to be taken to improve the odds in our favour. A loaf of bread mouldy with *Penicillium* is easily discarded, but a gallon of wine lost after some weeks is a tragedy.

Various sterilising and cleaning agents are on the market, produced especially for the homebrew hobby. Usually they are highly efficient chlorine- or soda-based preparations that will kill off any unwanted wildlife and leave your equipment spotlessly clean. They do have the disadvantage that it is usually advisable to rinse thoroughly afterwards to take away the smell left in the traces remaining after draining your bucket, demijohn etc.

The commonest, cheapest and most versatile sterilant is sulphur dioxide gas. This used to be produced by amateurs and professionals alike, by burning common flowers of sulphur in a metal ladle or bent spoon lowered carefully into the vat or barrel, where the choking fumes annihilated anything living therein. Nowadays the same efficient sterilising takes place, using the same sulphur dioxide gas, but it is produced by dissolving sodium metabisulphite in water. Potassium metabisulphite is almost as efficient and can be used as an alternative.

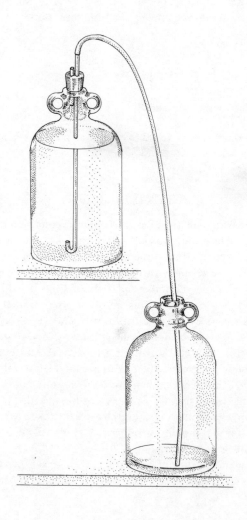

Naturally, winemakers quickly tired of talking about 'sodium metabisulphite' and the name was soon shortened to 'sulphite' – not accurate, but everyone in the hobby knows what it means. Sulphite was popularised in the early 1940s when sugar was in short supply, as a substance that could be used by housewives to preserve fruit in bottles for kitchen use out of season. In this form it was sold as Campden tablets and these pills are readily available from any homebrew supplier. Campden tablets lose strength once the container has been opened and many winemakers prefer to buy 2 oz (60 g) of sodium metabisulphite crystals and dissolve them in a pint (560 ml) of warm water. This is best done by putting the crystals or powder into a bottle with a screwcap, adding the water, replacing the cap, and shaking the bottle violently. The sulphite solution is quickly formed, without your lungs having suffered from the harsh and injurious sulphurous fumes. The solution can be transferred to a well-washed flexible detergent container. This makes the sulphite easy to dispense and, as long as the cap is fitted when the bottle is not in use, the contents will keep, ready for immediate use, for several months with little loss of strength. A good teaspoonful (6 g) of this solution is equal to one Campden tablet. This quantity in a gallon (4.5 litres) of water is sufficiently strong to sterilise fruit or rinse clean equipment, or it can be added undiluted to the must when it is being racked at various stages of its development.

Sulphite has three main roles to play. Initially it is used to sterilise equipment and to rinse fruit that is going to be fermented, in each case with the intention of wiping out or reducing considerably the spoilage agents that they naturally carry. When a must has been sulphited it is best left for 24 hours, by which time much of the sulphur dioxide will have dissipated into the air. The wine yeast you add has a certain sulphur tolerance and is thus able to build up a vast population before the spoilage yeasts or other unwanted organisms can recover. Thereafter, provided the air is excluded as soon as possible, and the must is kept covered in the meanwhile, there is no reason why your wine should not ferment out without off-flavours or bad bouquets.

The second role of sulphite when it is used as a sterilant is that part of the residual sulphur dioxide in the must becomes involved in the complex chemical changes concerned with the production of wine. This increases the amount of glycerol produced in the wine, with a resulting increase in smoothness and body. Wine should normally contain 1 – 2% of glycerol.

Thirdly, when the fermentation is virtually finished, the young wine should be racked off the sediment. A Campden tablet or a teaspoonful (5 ml) of 10% sulphite solution added at this stage not only helps as a yeast inhibitor, so activity slows and the wine starts clearing, but it is also an anti-oxidant. When you rack your wine, the turbulence gets rid of some of the dissolved fermentation gas (carbon dioxide), but the young wine picks up oxygen from the air. This will slowly cause the wine to brown, which can quite spoil a white wine. In extreme cases, or in wines exposed to a large air space due to a demijohn being only part-filled, the oxidation will actually spoil the wine's flavour, making it flat and uninteresting. The sulphur dioxide added combines with free oxygen and the wines survive unchanged.

CLOUDING AND HAZES

Because of the vast population of living yeast in a fermenting must it is to be expected, particularly in the early stages, that the must will usually be completely opaque. This is natural and, when the fermentation ends, the wine will slowly fall clear, from the surface downwards. However, for various reasons, wine can finish up with a decided hazy appearance and this is usually for one of three reasons. The first, and most obvious, is when a powdery yeast has been used; at each movement of the demijohn, clouds swirl up from the bottom of the jar. A good wine yeast does not usually react this way, being more likely to stick together to make a firm sediment. The cure here is self-evident: for the present, sulphite the must and rack again in a week's time. The prevention is simpler still – use a different strain of yeast in future.

Occasionally in wines that include starchy ingredients, such as grains or potatoes, or even apples, a slight persistent haze is apparent. This is caused by the starch, which is too complex a carbohydrate to be affected by the yeast. Starch in a must or wine is easily identified. Simply take a small quantity of wine and drip into it two or three drops of brown tincture of iodine. If starch is present there will be an instantaneous change of colour, a decided blue tinge appearing. In badly affected wines, this can be quite dramatic, a good deep blue resulting. Next time you have boiled potatoes at home, save some of the water in which the potatoes were cooked. When it is cool, add a few drops of iodine for a very convincing demonstration. The cure is to treat the must with an enzyme, variously known as diastase or (fungal) amylase, available from your suppliers. As preparations vary in strength, follow the manufacturer's instructions. Remember that most enzymes are inhibited by alcohol and, if you are treating a finished wine, you may find it necessary to add a little extra enzyme. Prevention lies in using non-starchy ingredients. If a recipe specifies a starchy ingredient, either don't break it up too finely or use hot water for the extraction.

The third and undoubtedly one of the commonest causes of hazy wine is pectin. It is also one of the easiest to prevent. Pectins are natural gummy substances found in most fruits, particularly stone fruits, such as the peach, apricot and plum, and of course apples, the major source of pectin sold for jam-making. Pectin is essential for making jam, as this is the substance that converts the boiled fruit and sugar into jam and allows it to set as a semi-solid. In winemaking, we do not want any pectin, for this semi-liquid substance forms a sort of diluted jelly throughout the wine, holding the yeast in suspension so that the wine will never clear properly. Any fruit that converts easily to jam, jelly or marmalade is high in pectin and should be treated accordingly.

All these fruits contain a natural enzyme, a pectinase, which will degrade the pectin. Alas, all enzymes are extremely susceptible to heat and are easily neutralised. It is advisable to add a pectin-destroying enzyme at the start of the must, allowing a little over the manufacturer's recommendations for fruits known to be heavy in pectin.

If you have doubts as to whether your must or wine contains pectin, this too is something for which there is a simple test. Using a small glass, half fill it with the liquid being tested, then add half as much of methylated spirits. If pectin is present, the two fluids won't mix and flecks and stringy blobs of coagulated pectin jelly will appear or, at the least, the methylated spirits will turn cloudy and opaque. In bad cases, the pectin may actually form an identifiable lump. Here the prevention is better than the cure, less enzyme being needed to break down the pectin in the bulk of the wine before it reaches its maximum alcohol content.

Apart from these two enzymic treatments, wines do occasionally need clearing and there are numerous proprietary preparations on sale. Most are based on isinglass, an extract of fish 'innards' cut with metabisulphite. This is simply stirred into the wine. Gelatine is used in a similar way, but in addition to clearing the wine also reduces the tannin content, so this has to be allowed for when using gelatine as a fining. It has proved useful in reducing the tannin content of some heavy fruit wines, as the alternative is to store the wine to mature, possibly for years, which also brings down the tannin content.

The remaining fining solution is one that contains chitin, which is extracted from the shells of lobsters and similar creatures. This is perhaps the most adaptable of all finings and seems to react well in most cases of haze.

There are other ways of fining your wines – a bucket of blood from the abattoir will fine a couple of hundred gallons (900 litres); even the white of a raw egg will clarify 10 – 20 gallons (45 – 90 litres). Casein is another clearing agent and I have heard of adventurous souls pouring milk into their cloudy wines, to fine them with casein. Generally speaking, isinglass or chitin are recommended as liquid additions.

However, there is another fining material used, a powdered montmorillonite clay known as Bentonite, after Fort Benton in Texas where it is, or was, mined. This remarkable clay is found in varying forms all over the world, being used for everything from a 'filler' for ladies' leg-tan makeup to heavy industrial filters. The clay has been subjected to great pressures and has a flat, layered construction. It will absorb quite a lot of water, forming a sort of gel, but unless previously treated cannot just be stirred into solution; it just forms sticky muddy lumps. Leave it to soak on its own for a day or two, (say a tablespoonful (20 g) of powder to 1 pint (560 ml) of water), giving it an occasional shake or stir to disperse the powder, and it will, unaided, form a beautiful silky gel. A tablespoonful (20ml) of this solution is normally sufficient to clear a gallon (4.5 litres) of wine, when well stirred in. Leave it for at least 2 or 3 days, up to a fortnight if you can. Best of all is to add a heaped teaspoonful (6 g) of dry powder to the newly made must. The currents set up in the fermentation will help to disperse the powder and no further action is necessary by the winemaker. Leave it a few days longer than usual before racking and the flocculent Bentonite sediment will settle down and become more compact, which of course means more drinkable wine can be syphoned. It is now also possible to buy Bentonite ready made as a gel (if you don't mind buying water) or as pre-treated granules that quickly disperse without difficulty.

Bentonite has one great advantage. Other types of fining, on odd occasions, may fix the haze instead of removing it. This does not happen with Bentonite. The only disadvantage is that, used to excess, it can give the wine an earthy taste; this seems to depend on the particular supply of Bentonite.

FILTRATION

A well-made wine, from a properly formulated recipe, should fall brilliantly clear without any intervention, as soon as the yeast has completed its work. Usually they do, but occasionally a wine will remain slightly hazy with yeast, or perhaps have tiny fragments of debris – 'floaters' in the parlance of judging – that obstinately will never settle as sediment. This is when some form of filtration is the only way of removing the offending particles. Or perhaps you are entering your wine in a competition and wish to polish it to that star-bright clarity the judge will be looking for. Here again, filtration is the answer.

Filters can be as simple as a freshly laundered and ironed linen cloth to a complex filter through which the wine is forced under pressure. The linen cloth removes small debris and little else. Next in efficiency come folded filter papers, resting in a funnel, and cellulose pulp supported in a filter paper or by a wad of coarse unmedicated cotton wool in a funnel. If you have neither, then you can use a piece of kitchen roll, but beware of other paper tissues; most of them smell of perfume that may be sweet to the nose but will ruin your wine.

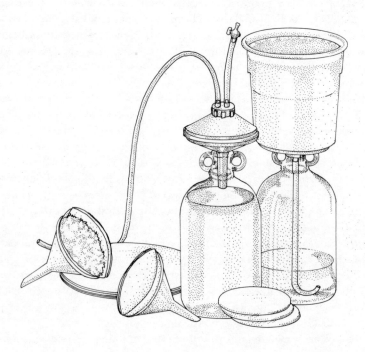

All these filter materials need to be well washed through with water, or the first pint or two of wine must be refiltered, to get rid of the myriads of tiny fragments of pulp that will make your wine look like a dust storm. Badly filtered wine is unmistakable, hundreds of tiny short hair-like bits drifting round as the bottle is rotated.

The commercial filters available at present are based on three main methods: filtration through pads of compressed filter medium, filtration through beds of caked powders supported by a special disc and filtration through a bag, on the inside of which settles filter medium stirred into the wine. All three work well and the selection of a filter is largely by price and personal preference. In each of these three types also, it is advisable to refilter the first pint or so of wine to remove odd hairs and dust washed through.

Many winemakers believe that filtration takes much more from a wine than just floaters; body, colour, flavour and even bouquet are all said to suffer. Whether or not this is so is unproven, but my own view is that, unless it is essential to filter wine, I do not filter it. As I said at the start of this section, wine should fall brilliantly clear and filtration will therefore only be required on odd occasions. If you do find that you have to filter, clear the wine beforehand with Bentonite and shake it well to release as much of the absorbed fermentation gas as possible. Gas in solution forms bubbles in the filter lines and blockages follow, preventing the wine from flowing. And do follow the manufacturer's instructions implicitly if you want the best results from your filter.

EXTRACTION

This is a vast subject, that could be expanded almost to a book on its own. Grape wine is made simply by crushing grapes and fermenting the resulting juice, or crushing red grapes, fermenting the juice and pulp, and then removing the pulp, skins etc. when the skins have provided sufficient pigment to make the wine red. Obviously these techniques wouldn't work with flowers, or hard fruits like apples or rose hips, or grains. So, as this book progresses through the seasons, techniques suitable for particular ingredients will be explained as they arise. Broadly however, they are as follows.

(1) **Pulp fermentation** This is the basic method. Crush the fruit, add all the other ingredients, water and yeast, ferment for a few days, and then strain or press out the fermenting juice. Normally pulp fermentation should not continue for more than a week, as there is a danger of wild yeasts, bacteria, or mildews attacking the pulp. Also, the rapid break-down of the fruit may mean you extract excessive amounts of tannins and other harsh substances that will spoil the flavour of your wine.

(2) **Juice extraction** Mechanical extraction, by using kitchen blenders, or electric or steam juicers, is now commonplace. Deep frozen fruit can be allowed to thaw and the juice is simply and efficiently extracted by using a press, or even by putting the softened fruit into a bag and pressing or squeezing it gently by hand.

(3) **Cooking** Some ingredients, for example root vegetables like parsnips and carrots, need scrubbing, cutting up coarsely, bringing slowly to the boil and simmering until just – and only just – tender when prodded with a fork. Excessive cooking softens the roots too much and the wine may become extremely hazy and probably most difficult to clear.

Remember, please, to use unsalted water! If you wish to eat the vegetables after the liquor has been strained off for winemaking, pour fresh boiling water over them, add salt and cook for a few minutes more.

Elderberries can be gently simmered for a few minutes. This softens the fruit for crushing, gives a more fruity-flavoured extract, but seems not to draw the tannins from the skins to the same extent as when pulp fermentation is the chosen method. The wine can therefore be drunk younger than would otherwise be the case. It is also advisable to simmer dried elderberries for a few minutes, for the same reasons.

Fruits like apples, that have a high pectin content, should not be cooked. Wines made from such extracts tend to be very hazy, almost opalescent, and taste just like cooked apple. These results are fine for apple pie, but not really suitable for what should be a brilliantly clear wine with a crisp, fresh flavour.

(4) **Soaking** This consists simply of crushing the fruit after sterilising it and soaking it in lightly sulphited water. This method extracts the best of the fruit flavour, as long as it does not extend beyond a week or, at most, 10 days.

(5) **Infusion** Flower wines, using just the petals, and herbal wines if they are not to be too strongly flavoured, can often best be made by soaking the flower petals or herbs in the fermenting wine, suspended in a muslin bag, with a couple of sterilised pebbles or glass marbles added to keep the bag submerged. Flower petals quickly decay and 24 hours is usually sufficient to extract from them the colour, bouquet, and flavour they provide. Heat should be avoided. Soaking them in a fermenting must means they are in the presence of alcohol, which as any perfumier will tell you, helps extract what is required and assists in retaining the extract in the must.

FERMENTATION

Once the extract, yeast, sugar etc. are safely in the demijohn, and under an airlock, it is largely just a matter of waiting until the fermentation ends. There are some points to be watched if a first-class wine is to be produced. The place where the fermentation takes place is important and should, ideally, have a steady temperature of around 70 – 75°F (21 – 24°C). Fluctuations cause the average temperature to vary, usually to a lower point, and the wine will take longer to ferment, though it may not be any the worse for that. Fermentation temperatures should not generally exceed 75°F (24°C) as higher temperatures mean a violent, frothy fermentation and many of the more delicate constituents that produce the better bouquets and flavours may be driven off and lost with the fermentation gases through the airlock.

When the pulp is strained or pressed to extract the juice or the fermenting must, almost invariably a certain amount of organic solids from the crushed fruit pass through into the fermenting jar. After a while, these will start to decay through their own enzymic action and off-flavours and smells will spoil the wine. To avoid this, it is advisable to rack the must off the thick sediment that forms in the demijohn after the first 10 or 15 days. Thereafter, unless for example, the recipe specifies that further sugar is to be added, the jar need not be disturbed again until the fermentation has ended.

At that point, when the airlock is no longer passing bubbles and the young wine is starting to fall clear, the wine is racked into a clean jar and a teaspoonful (5 ml) of sulphite solution or a crushed Campden tablet is added. This helps to clear the wine, reduces the chance of bacterial attack if it is a low alcohol wine and prevents oxidation.

MATURATION

After fermentation ends, the demijohn should be sealed with a cork bung or a piece of polythene and a strong elastic band. The elastic will stretch slightly and allow the excess gas to escape if the wine starts to ferment again. Do not use a solid rubber bung as, during storage, the surface of the bung may oxidise and weld itself to the neck of the demijohn. Should this happen and the wine re-ferments, the pressure from the carbon dioxide fermentation gas cannot blow the bung free and instead you will soon have a highly explosive glass demijohn. The injuries possible from such an explosion could be fatal, or crippling for life. Maturation should preferably be in a dark cool place, around 50°F (10°C). While the wine is maturing, it is slowly developing from a raw young wine into a wine with smoothness and elegance. The majority of home-made wines are drunk young, usually too young for their full potential to be realised. Wines can be, and are, drunk within a few weeks of the fermentation starting, and there are 2-week and 3-week wine kits on the market. But these descriptions refer only to the fermentation time, and a 3-week kit wine kept for a few months will almost certainly be a far pleasanter drink than one that has barely stopped bubbling. Young wines can be fresh and lively, fragrant and refreshing, and fun to drink. They would usually be much better for a little maturity. Beaujolais Nouveau and the Portuguese Vinho Verde are typical commercial examples.

Most homemade wines benefit greatly from being stored for a while out of bright light. In general, light white wines want keeping for 3 to 6 months, light reds for 6 to 12 months, and heavy sweet strong wines, red or white, for upwards of a year.

During its storage in bulk, subtle changes take place in the wine, Excess tannins combine with acids, reducing the harsh flavouring elements and producing the esters that will develop into the wine's bouquet. Young wine has an aroma normally of the principal ingredient, and one can easily identify rose petals, peaches or apples, for example, but, with time, this identifiable fruity aroma is muted and improved by the development of the wine. The wine thus becomes smoother and mellower, the flavour changes and improves, and the comparatively basic aroma changes to a distinctive bouquet. The whole is enhanced and develops into a much more complex and subtle liquid, reflecting the love, time and skill that have gone into producing it.

When the wine is stable, smooth and pleasing, then it may be time to bottle it. The wine should recover from this and be ready to drink within 2 or 3 weeks of rest.

This may seem a counsel of perfection and impossible to achieve if you are a new winemaker or have only small stocks. In such cases, most of your wine will be drunk young, but out of interest, make a few descriptive notes – honest ones – about the quality of your wine. Is it gassy, sharp, harsh, acidy, thin or cloudy? Put the notes away safely, take two of your precious half-dozen bottles, and store them away out of sight and out of temptation's way. Open one after 3 months and the other after 6 months and, each time, when you have drunk the wine, compare your opinion with your original notes. You will be surprised how much the wine mellows and improves.

BOTTLING

Bottling your wine is not difficult, though there are, as in everything, certain basic rules to be obeyed if your precious wine is going to be safely stored away until you wish to drink it.

Firstly, use only wine bottles. This sounds silly, but I have seen wine in sauce bottles, whisky and gin bottles and various other unsuitable containers. If you can't obtain enough wine bottles, then rack the wine straight from the demijohn into a carafe or decanter. This does mean that the whole gallon will have to be drunk fairly quickly to avoid deterioration, but this doesn't usually seem to be much of a problem. If you can bottle your wine in the same style of bottle used for its commercial equivalent, e.g. a long tapering green or brown bottle for a light German-type white table wine, then it will be aesthetically all the more acceptable. A wine well bottled, neatly labelled and properly stoppered, looks far more attractive than the same wine scruffily presented and, because it is visually pleasing, it usually tastes better too.

Rack your mature wine off any sediment that has formed and add a teaspoonful (5 ml) of sulphite per gallon (4.5 litres). The bottles should be free from cracks, chips or scars, scrupulously clean and sterilised. A bottle brush makes the task of cleaning bottles much easier, especially when combined with a proprietary cleaning agent.

Before you start bottling the wine, soak sufficient corks or stoppers in a pint (560 ml) of hot water with a teaspoonful (5 ml) of sulphite solution. If this is put in a pudding basin, a saucer can be placed on top of the corks to keep them submerged. After about 20 minutes, squeeze the corks under a running tap to wash out any cork dust remaining in the crevices. Long cylindrical corks are needed if the wine is to be laid down in a wine rack to mature in bottle. Short mushroom-shaped stoppers can be used if the bottle is to be stored upright for a limited period. They are not suitable for long-term storage as they dry out and allow bacteria to enter the wine if

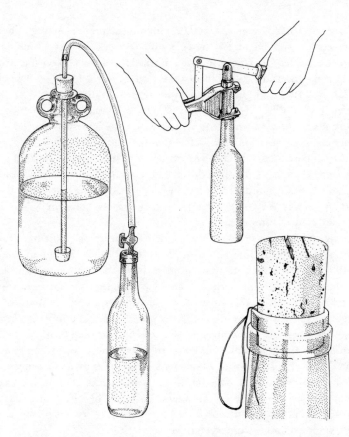

the bottles are stored upright. They do not usually have sufficient grip on the bottle for it to be safely stored at an angle in a wine rack, where the wine prevents the cork from drying out. Short stoppers easily blow out of the bottles and some, if not all, of the contents can be lost by spillage and contamination.

Syphon the wine gently, without any avoidable splashing, into the bottles; the air-space remaining in the bottle neck should be between 1¾ – 2¼ inches (4.5 – 5.5 cm), depending on whether short stoppers or long cylindrical corks are used. To fit the corks, hang a small piece of fine hard string or nylon over the rim of the bottle, so that it hangs down inside and out. Drive home the stopper by hand, or the

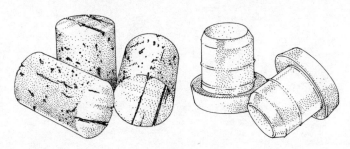

long cork by using a corking gun, and then pull out the piece of string. This releases the compressed air trapped under the cork and reduces the risk of the cork being blown from the bottle. Corking guns vary in design, but work on the principle of compressing the cork and driving it into the bottle with a plunger. The cork then expands slightly to make a tight fit in the tapering neck of the bottle.

Decorative and descriptive wine labels are available for homemade wines, together with neck labels on which the year in which the wine was started is entered. Many labels are not pre-gummed, as the slightest humidity can weld them into a block of waste paper. Such labels can be attached to the bottle with solid glue sticks or wallpaper paste, in fact with any adhesive that is not too difficult to remove when the bottle is eventually emptied and ready for washing again. Even the rubber cement out of a bicycle tyre repair kit, or carpet latex solution will prove quite satisfactory and easy to remove later.

The final decorative touch for dressing a bottle is to fit a capsule over the cork or stopper. There are several different types, the commonest being of aluminium foil, applied with a thick rubber ring that is rolled down the bottle neck and up again. Shrink-on capsules are usually either of heavy plastic that softens in hot water and can be stretched over the bottle before they cool and tighten up, or made of a special plastic that shrinks tightly onto the bottle neck when heat is applied to it. All come in a variety of colours and give your bottles a neat professional finish.

Commercial wines are now also sold in cartons with non-porous liners and with a small integral tap. These 'bag-in-a-box' wines can be drawn off over a period of some weeks without noticeable deterioration, as air cannot get into the bag to spoil the contents. Similar collapsible containers, such as the 'Vincanter' are sold at homebrew supply shops and are an excellent substitute for bottles in the case of wines which will be drunk within a relatively short time.

Serving Your Wines

We now approach the point at which it is easy to become excessively twee or to be branded as a wine snob. But basically the following points are to ensure that you

gain the most enjoyment from the wine you have laboured to produce, and are simply putting into words what hundreds of years of wine drinking has taught millions of thirsty wine-bibbers and wine-lovers. Obviously, it your wine is barely a month old it will be undeveloped, but if you have nothing else then of course you will drink it, and presenting it pleasingly is as important as bottling it attractively. If it is a venerable old wine you have treasured, then showing it respect in the way you serve it is equally necessary in order to gain the maximum enjoyment from it.

Let us again look firstly at table wines. Light white wines generally taste crisper and brighter when they are chilled; an hour in the door of the refrigerator is sufficient. If you don't have refrigeration, drape a wet cloth over the bottle, stand it in a draught and the evaporation will cool it reasonably well on a hot day. Please don't be tempted to put your wine in a deep-freeze cabinet. Really cold wine simply numbs the palate and one might as well drink icewater.

Rosé wines vary, as a few resemble red wines in all except colour. The majority, however, are light, crisp wines and are better chilled than not.

Red wines do not usually respond well to chilling, unless they are being used as part of a long drink, like a sangria or fruit cup. Red wines are normally served at room temperature, releasing the bouquet so that one is aware of the pleasure of the wine, and even its quality, before tasting it. The flavour of red wine tends to be more complex than that of white and can be more easily enjoyed if not too cold.

None of these are rules, of course; the only rule about wine is to drink what you like when you like. This applies equally well to the conventions of what wines go with which foods. These guides are simply what experience has shown to suit most people. As practical examples, one would not normally drink a thin acid Rheinwein with a rich sweet dessert – it would be like drinking vinegar. But the same wine with a piece of cold chicken and a salad would probably be most enjoyable. Similarly a good strong red wine that would perfectly complement a grilled steak would taste harsh and metallic, and full of tannin, if drunk while eating a fish dish such as cod or whiting. So rules they are not, just recommendations based on what most people have found most pleasing. The main thing is to drink what you enjoy and to enjoy it when you drink it.

Next to consider is the use of wine baskets. If you have a vintage port that has been laid down, white spot uppermost, for months or years, or any other old wine that has thrown a deposit, then carrying it in a wine basket will make it easier to draw the cork and decant the wine without disturbing that longstanding 'crust' or sediment. Apart from that, such baskets merely look decorative and cause a bottle of wine to take up four times the table space it should do. If you do plan on serving a wine that has thrown a sediment, then gently standing it upright a day or two beforehand will make carrying it and decanting it easier still, as the crust should slide gently down into the punt (the 'kick-up' or indentation in the base) of the bottle. Decanting, by the way, is simply pouring the wine very quietly and steadily into a fresh container so that the sediment is not carried over with it, to spoil the clarity of the wine.

Glasses are necessary to enjoy wine; it just does not taste the same out of a coffee mug or a plastic tumbler. Standard glasses such as publicans use are known as Paris goblets, and they will suffice for most wines. If you wish to extend your range of glasses then you have plenty from which to choose. It is great fun and even inexpensive glassware can be very varied and attractive. If you want to show off your wines, don't load your shelves with coloured or patterned glasses, as these detract from the visual effect of a clear well-coloured wine, with lights glinting in it.

One last point: extracting the cork. It is not advisable to use one of those gadgets that inject air or gas through a needle that pierces the cork, as bottles, particularly old or re-used bottles, as yours certainly will be before long, may burst or split under the pressure generated to push the cork out. If nothing worse, it's a terrible waste of wine. If you can find one, the 'Screwpull' is dearer than most, but highly efficient and foolproof. Most of the double-arm lever-type work well and, for a portable corkscrew, the standard pattern of 'waiter's friend' is quite satisfactory. The latter usually incorporates a small blade to cut the capsule and some have a crown-cork lifter for opening beer-bottles too. A poor corkscrew will break corks, pull holes through them and generally drive you to drink – if you can get one!

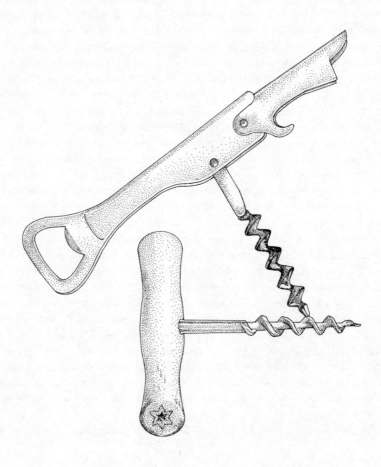

BEER AND BREWING

Beer, that staple drink of Western man, drunk wherever he has colonised, is actually a very ancient beverage. Some 5000 years ago, the Babylonians of Mesopotamia were malting barley and emmer (a primitive wheat), fermenting the extract and happily drinking the herb-flavoured result. The ancient Egyptians were quick to follow suit, fermenting barley and wheat and coining suitably sounding words, like *bouzah*. Remarkably, both nations discovered ways of preserving malt for times when beer supplies were running low. The Babylonians made a malt extract for brewing, then boiled it to evaporate the water to leave a thick syrup. In Egypt, the problem was solved in a different way, by lightly baking loaves of coarse flour that remained moist inside. In both instances, these primitive 'beer kits' could easily be used as the base for a fermentation with little delay.

Historically, the fermented extract of malted grain has been known as 'ale', a bland drink with poor keeping qualities. Many and varied herbs were used to flavour ales and to try and preserve them. Bog myrtle, ivy, lichen from oak trees and many others have been tried, with even the Church in Europe holding the monopoly of a herbal blend called *gruit*.

But the ideal herb for flavouring, disinfecting and preserving the brew proved eventually to be the hop *(Humulus lupulus)*, which was grown in Germany at least as early as the eighth century. By the fifteenth century, its use had spread across Europe and reached England through Holland. This new drink, called 'beer', met great opposition from the brewers of the traditional ales, but slowly and surely its clean taste and economic superiority drove the old ales from the market. It took over a hundred years, but eventually beer reigned supreme.

Ale and beer had traditionally been brewed firstly by the women of each household and then, more commonly, by brewers who supplied other houses, public and private. In the eighteenth century, the big breweries were founded – Truman, Whitbread and Guinness are examples – and from then until the current day there has been a continuing reduction in the number of brewers and, in consequence, in the range and variety of beers on sale.

This trend was so marked in the 1950s and 1960s that, in 1971 the Campaign for Real Ale (CAMRA) was founded and this voluntary body has successfully fought, on behalf of all British beerdrinkers, and unending war on the restrictive practices of the six major combines, who between them control over 75% of Britain's beer. Many small breweries have survived and still produce their distinctive brews, numerous new small independents have started brewing, and all this has helped make the average drinker much more conscious of the great variation in flavour and style possible in this beverage.

This, together with the standardisation of the fizzy keg beers, acidified with carbon dioxide gas, sold by the majority of publicans, has helped to popularise homebrewing for the amateur. Many people have taken up the hobby simply because of the excessive prices charged for commercial beers, particularly the heavily advertised lagers, but many more make their own beers just for the pleasure of having full-bodied drinks, aromatic with ample hops and tasting of malt, instead of the thin, low alcohol brews so often sold. Even the homebrewer who uses only the standardised kits on sale will produce beers of greater character and interest than many of the beers available from the big breweries.

The brewers have learned, from CAMRA and from falling sales, that high prices and low quality are unacceptable, and are installing handpull beer engines and 'real ales' in many pubs and clubs. In the meantime, the homebrew hobby has been given such a boost in growth that it seems likely that it will be many years, if ever, before the brewers need no longer worry about it and the lost trade it represents.

In addition, several other factors have helped popularise amateur brewing. Previously mentioned, Reginald Maudling's action as Chancellor of the Exchequer in freeing homebrewing from licensing restraints has since been followed by popularised television, road safety campaigns and breathalyser legislation that encourage drinking at home. This, the abolition of retail price maintenance and the growth in the range of drinks available from the increasing number of supermarkets and other off-licence sales outlets have all tended to take drinkers away from the public houses and clubs. And once the practice of drinking at home is accepted, then making an experimental gallon of beer frequently follows. After that, homebrewing often becomes another interest to be followed, a rewarding and fulfilling hobby.

There are two great advantages that the homebrewer has over the home winemaker. Firstly, most beers are fermented and cleared in about 7 days and can then be bottled or barrelled. Maturing usually takes no more than 3 weeks, by which time the beer, if bottled, has undergone a secondary fermentation and has reached a smooth and satisfying readiness for drinking or, if casked, will be ready to be drawn off, clear and sparkling, to be admired by the eye and then enjoyed as a drink.

Secondly, whereas the amateur winemaker is usually handicapped by the availability of his ingredients compared with the professional vintner, the homebrewer uses precisely the same materials as the professional brewer: hops, malted barley, yeast and water. There are also several other ingredients that can be used, such as brewing flour, flaked rice and maize, and wheat or barley syrups, which are also available to the amateur, though some are not in every shop.

A natural and inevitable accompaniment to the growth of our hobby was the development and expansion of the trade to support and supply it. Beer kits proliferated and new brands and varieties are continually being introduced.

Because of the greatly increased demand, the retail outlets for hops, malts and other ingredients became more numerous and better quality supplies came on the market, which had the feed-back effect of making it possible for homebrewers to produce even better beers. This again called for increased technical knowledge and several exceedingly good books of great interest to specialist amateur brewers have been published, in addition to many books and articles of simpler recipes and techniques. The homebrewer has never been better catered for and no one now need lack a constant supply of excellent beers of his or her own making.

Equipment

Beer-brewing calls for a small and simple range of equipment, but preferably capable of handling several gallons (9 litres or so) of liquid. Beers can be, and indeed are, brewed in 1-gallon (4.5 litre) batches, but as a gallon is only 8 pints (8 × 560 ml), it is hardly worth the effort. Five gallons (22.5 litres) can be brewed just as easily as one and, as the old saying goes, last twice as long.

Beer is made by extracting fermentable sugars from malted grain, boiling the extract with hops, and fermenting the cooled wort (pronounced like 'curt', not 'bought') with a yeast. The beer is then barrelled, for a draught beer, or bottled or put in some other pressurised container, for sparkling beer.

To make beer at home, from a simple commercial 'kit' of hopped malt extract, calls for the use of an enamel, aluminium, or stainless steel pan, preferably one that will hold at least a gallon (4.5 litres), a white or clear plastic bucket with a close-fitting lid and a long-handled spoon or hardwood rod for stirring. In addition, you will need a tin opener and a tablespoon.

Following a recipe that uses hops and malt grains will also entail the use of a sieve or colander capable of holding several pounds (over a kilogram) of solids.

Finally, the fermented beer has to be bottled or put in a pressure barrel to condition and mature, to give you a beautiful sparkling golden drink.

In addition to the bottles, you will need a syphon tube, bottletops, such as crown corks, and a capping tool to fit them with. Draught beer is usually stored in a plastic barrel with a specially adapted cap to take a metal bottle of carbon dioxide. This gas helps keep the beer sparkling bright and prevents infection by airborne wild yeasts and bacteria.

Ingredients

WATER

The major part of any beer, known to the trade as liquor, is water. The varying degrees of temporary or permanent hardness in water, due to the amounts and types of dissolved minerals, predispose the water to make a particular type of beer best. Because of this, certain places became famous for different types of beer, like the milds and brown ales of London and the pale ales of Burton on Trent. Nowadays, the brewery chemists adapt the available water supply to suit the type of beer being brewed. Brewing salts are on sale to amateur brewers, but need only be considered if you live in a 'soft'-water area, i.e. where the temporary hardness is largely lost in boiling, and you intend to make light-coloured hoppier beers, such as pale lagers and bitters. For most British brewers, as long as you are not intensely competition-minded, the water supply is not of any great consequence, providing the supply remains pure and uncontaminated.

MALT

Unlike winemaking, where the yeast has a readily accessible supply of sugar, brewing uses barley grain as the raw material. As with most seeds, the energy is stored in the form of starch, which yeast cannot utilise. This starch is modified to sugars by enzymes when the seed starts growing and needs food to develop. Barley for brewing is therefore artificially stimulated into growth by spraying it with water on a warm dark malthouse floor. As the growing shoot appears from the seed, the starch is partly converted to sugar and unused enzymes are held ready to continue the process. At this point, the grain is dried and partly roasted in a kiln, which arrests the growth of the embryo plant. This is the process of 'malting' the grain. Malted barley is kilned to varying degrees, from very pale malts, produced for lagers and pale ales, through to crystal malt, in which the starch is completely converted to sugar that caramelises into crystals. Crystal malt has no active enzyme left in it and the sugar can be extracted simply by boiling the crushed grain. Once popular as part of the formulation for stouts, 'patent black malt' is malt that has been roasted until the sugar has almost burned away, leaving the malt with a harsh flavour. Nowadays, most brewers substitute roasted barley, which is unmalted grain roasted to give the stout a suitable colour and flavour. The 'patent' expired many years ago, but the name lingers on.

To avoid the need for the amateur to undertake the skilled process of mashing the grain, this is now done professionally and the resulting malt extract is a thick syrup ready for immediate use. Malt extract is available in varying grades to match the grade of roast of malted barley it was extracted from.

This process has been taken yet one step further and malt extract can be bought as a powder. This powder is hygroscopic; i.e. it will take up water, or even moisture from the air, very quickly and, unless kept sealed in polythene bags, will rapidly turn back into a sticky toffee-like substance. This does not affect the value of the malt, but makes it quite difficult to handle.

Dried malt extract, weight for weight, is approximately one fifth higher in value as a brewing material than malt extract in syrup form.

HOPS

A relative of the cannabis plant, the hop grows wild in southern England, but for the home-brewer only the commercially grown hop is reliable and consistent in its preservative and flavouring content.

The hop is a perennial plant, each year throwing up rambling stalks or bines that curl clockwise up guide wires in the hopyards. The hop that is harvested is the female flower cone, which is carefully dried and stored until sold, in 'pockets' – tall sacks holding 1½ cwt (about 76 kg) or, as the Common Market names it, 1½ zentners. Hops contain two particular substances, humulin and lupulin, which are referred to as alpha and beta acid. Most hops are graded by their alpha acid content and this is why the old-fashioned low-acid hops, such as Fuggles and Goldings, are slowly being replaced by more modern varieties, such as Bramling Cross and the Whitbread Golding Variety. Several hop varieties are now on sale, including Continental hops like Saaz and Hallertauer. Less is needed of the Continentals for the simple reason that, in mainland Europe, the male hop plant has been virtually eradicated. In consequence, the female plants do not set seed and you get more hops for your money just because they weigh less.

Hops in good condition should be a pale green, resilient to the touch and containing a bright orange-yellow powder. If the hops are pale yellow and brittle and the bag has a lot of broken bits and dust in the bottom, the hops are old and should be rejected. They would give your beer little but a coarse bitterness and poor aroma.

Most suppliers now stock hop-oil extracts. These are not really suitable as a replacement for hops in a good beer, but a drop or two added to an otherwise dull beer can improve the nose and flavour of the brew.

Hops provide the bitter flavour of beer, give the drink a clean fresh bouquet and act as a preservative after fermentation. When the barley malt has been mashed, or the extract dissolved, the hops are boiled with the wort. This extracts the valuable resins and oils from the hops, and the solids that are left are used as a filter bed for the wort. After being sprayed with hot water to wash out the malt solution they hold, a process known as 'sparging', the spent hops are discarded, sometimes being sold by breweries for use as gardener's compost or mulch.

YEAST

There are two major strains of yeast: *Sacccharomyces cerevisiae*, the brewers' yeast used in the United Kingdom for fermenting beer, and *S. carlsbergensis*, used by most of the rest of the world for brewing lagers and similar beers.

The British brewer's yeast is known as a 'top-fermenting' yeast, because although the whole of the wort is turbid with yeast, a great surplus of yeast is thrown out on the surface of the beer, rather like a frothy soft meringue, where it piles up as 'rocky heads'. This surplus yeast should be skimmed off and discarded, to prevent it sinking back into the beer and spoiling the flavour. So much surplus yeast is produced by breweries that it is sold for conversion to yeast tablets, savoury yeast extract spreads and other products.

Lager and other beers brewed abroad use what is known as a 'bottom-fermenting' yeast. Here, too, the whole of the liquid is clouded with yeast and a small amount of yeast is thrown up at the surface. Most of the yeast sinks to the bottom of the fermenting vessel and remains active as long as there is fermentable sugar (maltose) in the brew. Lager yeasts tend to ferment more slowly, at lower temperatures and for a longer time than top-fermenting yeasts. The yeast is so important in brewing that a fresh yeast should be 'pitched' (added to the cooled wort) each time you brew.

ADJUNCTS

Adjuncts are unmalted materials used to modify the body or flavour of a beer or to extend an expensive malt. Most good malts contain more of the starch-converting enzymes than needed for that ingredient. Thus other starchy materials can be used at low cost in the knowledge that the malt enzymes will convert the starch in the adjunct as well as in the malt.

Other 'grits' are commonly used, such as rice flour, kibbled (broken) wheat and maize, and various cereal products.

Also there are syrups produced from wheat and other grains that have been chemically changed from starches to sugars and these syrups are readily fermentable. They do, however, ferment away almost completely and, if used in too high a proportion, tend to make the beer thin.

Roasted barley, previously mentioned, is unmalted barley grain that has in effect been oven-browned. If your supplier does not stock this ingredient, plain whole barley is easily roasted in a large metal dish in your kitchen oven if you wish to attempt an Irish-type stout.

FINING

Being made of a starchy and proteinaceous material, beer occasionally remains stubbornly cloudy. This can often be prevented by adding carragheen seaweed, better known as 'copper finings' or 'Irish moss' to the boil at the rate of about a ¼ teaspoonful (1.5 g) to a 5-gallon (22.5 litres) brew, or according to the supplier's directions. Irish moss helps to clear the beer by coagulating proteins, which settle out as the wort cools.

When the fermentation ends, the yeast should sink, leaving a clear bright beer behind. Sometimes it remains hazy and proprietary finings of isinglass or chitin should be stirred in and the beer left for 24 hours. It will usually then be ready for racking and either bottling or kegging. As finings vary enormously, I can only advise that you use the dosage recommended by the manufacturer.

The Brewing Process

The very first consideration in brewing is the sterilisation of equipment. The ingredients themselves are usually brought to the boil or dissolved in hot water and canned malt extracts are, of course, sterile to start with. Such heat treatment is sufficient to sterilise the ingredients, but hot water alone is not enough to kill off the wild yeasts and other miscroscopic lifeforms in the buckets, syphon tubes, bottles and barrels and other equipment we use. For physically cleaning your equipment, there are proprietary cleaners, either chlorine-based, such as Chempro, or alkalis such as Silana P.F. Whatever cleaner you employ, the equipment should be well rinsed before use to avoid any affect on the nose or taste of the finished beer. What is very important is that you should not use soaps or ordinary household detergents as these will destroy the head on your beer. Such cleaning substances reduce surface tension and so the rising bubbles burst instead of producing that lasting collar of froth that adds to the texture and eye appeal of a good glass of beer.

Proprietary cleaners are excellent for removing stains and the dull film that slowly accumulates and makes buckets and bottles look dowdy, and for cleaning inside barrels and other dark and hidden corners.

To bring these cleaned items to a suitable state for brewing, or containing the finished beer, all that is needed is sulphur dioxide, in the form of Campden tablets, sodium metabisulphite or potassium metabisulphite. This is fully covered on pages 21 – 23 in the section on winemaking and the rules set down there apply equally to brewing. Beer is a comparatively low alcohol drink and is, therefore, particularly susceptible to infections. It is most important that it is protected as far as possible by sulphur dioxide, plus a close-fitting lid during the early stages of the fermentation and an airlock in the later stages.

When making kit beers, the instructions on the can or box are usually explicit, but do not always include bringing the brew to the boil. This is recommended and, as the sugar to be added needs dissolving in hot water, causes little extra work. When heating the malt extract syrup, it should be gently but frequently stirred or it will burn slightly. Burning the malt darkens the beer and gives it a burnt caramel flavour.

Beers made from recipes where the ingredients are bought separately also need boiling for a short period. Malt extract beers only require 20 minutes or so to extract the flavour and preservatives from the hops and to ensure the malt is thoroughly dissolved and blended with the extract from the hops. Grain beers, i.e. those made with crushed malted barley that has not been reduced to an extract, have to be simmered for roughly an hour at 150°F (65°C), within a degree or so, in the form of a thin porridge. This enables the diastatic enzymes to continue the process of converting complex starch carbohydrates to simple maltose sugars and dextrins that the yeast will be able to ferment. Mashing a little below this temperature gives a higher proportion of dextrins, the slow-fermenting sugars that give the beer body and head-forming ability. Higher temperatures increase the proportion of maltose, the sugar that is quickly fermented by the yeast, leaving a thin over-attenuated beer.

A grain mash needs testing periodically to check whether all the starch has been converted to sugar. This is simply done by spotting a few drops of the mash liquid onto a white surface, a tile or saucer for instance, and then adding a drop or two of brown tincture of iodine. If starch is still present, a distinct blue colour will appear, varying in depth from a deep navy blue if there is a lot of starch, to a pale thin blue showing that the mashing period has almost come to an end. Cooking the mash at too high a temperature will inactivate the enzymes and conversion does not take place. Residual starch when the mashing process has ended means that the beer may be hazy, particularly if chilled, and will be weaker than it should be for the quantity of ingredients used.

After the mashing the mash has to be strained and the broken husks of the barley retained in the sieve or straining cloth. A great deal of the fermentable sugar solution is trapped in the husks and requires washing out into the fermenting bin by spraying with hot water. This process is known as sparging. The liquor is returned to the pan and boiled with the hops for an hour and finally strained off the spent hop cones. Cooling should take place quickly, to assist in coagulating and sedimenting the proteins in the wort. This is most simply carrried out by adding cold water to bring the wort up to the correct final volume for the brew.

When the temperature drops to 70°F (21°C), the yeast is sprinkled on the surface of the wort and the lid or covering cloth replaced. Within 24 hours the beer should be actively and visibly fermenting and, a day later still, the fermentation should be heavily under way and starting to throw up the stiff foam that is largely surplus yeast.

This excess needs skimming off and discarding. At the same time, you will see a 'tide-line' of dark brown sticky substance ringing the bin at surface level. Wipe this off with a clean cloth as it is partly surplus yeast and partly coarse and bitter hop resins that would detract from the flavour of the beer.

After 3 or 4 days, the fermentation starts to slow down and no further yeast is thrown up as surface foam. At this point, it is good practice to syphon the wort into another container that can have an airlock fitted, to protect the beer from infection. In the first few days of lively active fermentation, the yeast produces a lot of carbon dioxide gas and, as this is heavier than air, it forms a protective blanket over the wort. This prevents the wild film yeasts from attacking the young beer, as they need air to multiply. When the fermentation slows down, the beer is still comparatively low in alcohol and susceptible to infection. As the carbon dioxide and foam production are reduced, the beer benefits from the protection of an airlock until fermentation ends and the beer is made.

At that point, finings can be added in accordance with the maker's instructions; isinglass or chitin finings are preferable. A day later, the beer should be clear and ready for racking off the sediment and bottling or barrelling.

Bottling beer has points for and against it. The main disadvantages are in having to acquire sufficient bottles and in cleaning them for use. Accumulating bottles is best done by buying bottled beer and drinking the contents, or you may find a friendly supplier who will provide bottles for just the deposit. Do not be tempted into using non-returnable or no-deposit bottles as these are of thin glass that is fragile and are not meant to be refilled. For your own safety, these bottles should be scrapped. Apart from this, any bottle that has been made to contain fizzy drinks is satisfactory: you can bottle your beer in any sort of fizzy pop bottle. Plastic screw caps and new washers are available. Even the PET-plastic beer and soft drinks bottles are safely reusable. These usually have a black plastic base and have a capacity of 1½ or 2 litres (about 2½ or 3½ pints).

Standard glass beer bottles are mostly sealed by crown corks crimped on by machine. These small metal caps can be bought quite cleaply from any homebrew supplier and are easily fitted by a knock-on capping tool struck by a hammer or a proper hand-capping machine that holds the crown with a magnet and presses it onto the bottle neck by leverage. Such tools are available for just a few pounds and

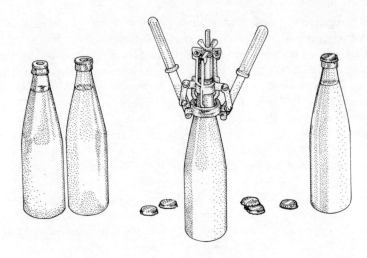

will last for years. There are reusable plastic clip-on caps that also fit ordinary crown bottles, but these tend to harden with use, leading to lack of gas-tightness and flat beers in consequence. Even a grain of sugar can cause one of these caps to fail. They are handy for resealing a bottle when only part of its contents are being used.

Bottled beer relies on a small re-fermentation in the bottle to provide a little gas in solution when the beer is opened. A little extra sugar is added at the bottling stage for this secondary fermentation. This carbon dioxide gives the beer a sparkle and is released as strings of bubbles that should rise in the beer glass for half an hour or so. These pile up at the surface as froth. The gas in solution is referred to as the 'condition' of the beer and the froth is the 'head'. The head should last as long as the drink and some froth should stick to the sides of the glass when the beer is gone. For a good example of a beer head, try a glass of Guinness stout, preferably bottled. Note the fine head, or bubbles, and the way the long-lasting head clings to the glass. As mentioned previously, detergents and soaps will spoil the head on a glass of beer, and you may have noticed when eating a 'ploughman's lunch' of cheese and bread and butter, how the head on your beer quickly disperses. This is due to the fats in your meal being transferred to the glass when you drink from it. A similar effect may be found when glasses have been in a domestic dishwasher, where a finishing agent is added to prevent the dishes showing streaks when dry, or even when hand-washed glasses, well rinsed in clean water, are dried with a tea-towel that still bears traces of detergent washing powder. Conditioning beer in the bottle inevitably results in a slight deposit of yeast. To avoid your drink being cloudy when served, decant all the beer into a jug at one pouring or fill sufficient glasses at one time. Tilting the bottle backwards and forwards causes turbulence that stirs up the deposit and spoils the appearance of the beer for another half day at least.

Draught beer is usually stored in a plastic barrel or a stainless steel keg, though the latter is not usually in the equipment of the occasional brewer. The common practice is to rack the clear beer into a plastic barrel, add the priming sugar (i.e. the sugar necessary for the secondary fermentation to condition the beer) and screw down the lid. After a week or two, clear beer can be run off from the tap. After a few glasses, the flow will slow down and air will start to be sucked into the barrel to replace the beer. This is an obvious source of infection and the beer will soon deteriorate. If you are throwing a party where most of the beer will be drunk within a short time, the cap can be slackened to admit air and all will be well. On the other hand, if you have brewed 5 gallons (22.5 litres) and just like an occasional drink or two with a friend, then it is advisable to use a barrel fitted with a special cap to take a bottle of carbon dioxide gas, either the small metal containers used to charge soda syphons or, preferably, the refillable bottle sold for the purpose. This extra gas does not pressurise the barrel to drive the beer through the tap, as is the case with most keg beer in public houses, but keeps a sterile atmosphere over the beer so that it does not deteriorate or turn to vinegar.

Beer is a wonderful beverage and producing it can be just a simple exercise for the thirsty man or woman who wants to make a clean-flavoured sparkling and satisfying brew at home or a complex operation for the enthusiast who wishes to delve into detail in the same way as the commercial brewers and brew beer to the same exacting standards. Either way, you will be well pleased with the finished product.

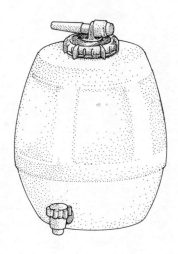

SPRING

After the long desolate months of Winter have dragged past, everyone's heart is lightened by the flowers of Spring. Snowdrops and crocuses brave the frosts to bring beauty and colour to the world, and are quickly followed by daffodils and narcissi in a variety of shapes and shades and tulips, with bold bright colours and patterns, standing proudly and stiffly to attention. Sweetly scented hyacinths and their small imitators, the bright blue grape hyacinths, complete the list of popular and common Spring bulbs. How beautiful they are, and how disappointing to the winemaker, for there is not a fermentable flower in the lot! Indeed, some will make you quite ill if consumed.

So enjoy the bright and attractive flowers, take pleasure in the nodding blooms in your flowerbeds, and look elsewhere for your wine-making ingredients.

Silver Birch

Before the Spring blossoms appear, the sap starts to rise in the deciduous trees, bringing new life in the form of dissolved minerals and nutrients to feed the growing buds and expanding leaves. One tree with a particularly vigorous sap flow at the end of March is the silver birch and this sap can be used as the base for a distinctive but enjoyable wine. It is necessary to tap the tree to obtain the sap, but providing the tree is at least 8 or 9 inches (20 or 23 cm) in diameter, and the hole is firmly plugged afterwards, the tree will come to no harm.

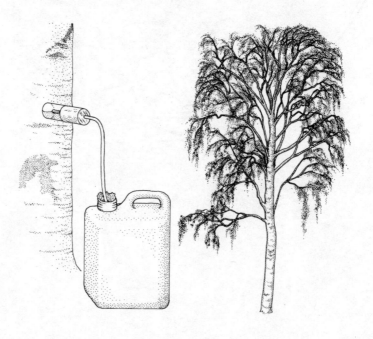

The sap rises through the thin outside layer of living wood just under the silvery bark, so it is only necessary to drill a short way into the tree. A ⅞ inch (2 cm) drill bit is a convenient size to use as a bored standard wine bottle cork can be fitted into the hole it makes. The cork holds a length of plastic tubing (see page 00) that leads the sap from the tree to a waiting container. Plugging the neck of the container with a chunk of foam rubber helps to keep the collected sap clean and free from insects.

If the time is right, the sap will start to drip down the tree trunk as soon as the drill bit cuts into it. A good tree in full flow can give you a gallon (4.5 litres) of sap a day, but half this quantity is probably average. After you have taken a couple of gallons (9 litres) from a tree it should be plugged with a solid cork. This will keep out the spores of fungus and mould that might harm the tree, but will be compressed by the fresh bark that will slowly grow and seal the hole.

BIRCH SAP WINE

2 medium-sized oranges
2 ¼ lb (1 kg) granulated sugar
6 pints (3.4 litres) birch sap (add water if necessary)
8 oz (225 g) minced sultanas (or 6 fl.oz/170 ml can of white grape concentrate)
1 cup strong tea
1 teaspoon (5 g) pectic enzyme
1 heaped teaspoon (6 g) Bentonite powder
Wine yeast

Squeeze the juice from the oranges, then scrape the coloured part of the peel – the zest – off the white pith and put the juice and zest in a large pan. Throw away the pith as this has a bitter flavour. Add the sugar, sap, sultanas and tea to the pan and bring to the boil. Simmer for 10 or 15 minutes, then pour through a fine strainer into a sterilised plastic bucket. Fit the lid or cover tightly and leave the must to cool.

When the temperature has dropped to 70°F (21°C), pour through a funnel into a demijohn and add the pectic enzyme, Bentonite and yeast. Top the jar up to the shoulder with cold water. Fit an airlock to a rubber bung, push the bung into the neck of the demijohn and half-fill the airlock with water. Refit the lid or dust-cap.

Keep the demijohn at room temperature or above, between 70 and 80°F (21 and 26°C). The fermentation should be under way within 48 hours and will first appear as a clouding of the wine and minute bubbles that rise to the surface when the demijohn is disturbed. Tiny gas bubbles can also be seen in the meniscus, which is where the surface tension of the must pulls the edge of the wine up the glass. Large bubbles should soon start blowing through the airlock.

When the fermentation has ended, the airlock will be still and the wine will start clearing from the surface downwards. Place the wine in a cool place. If it is not completely clear within a week, add wine finings according to the maker's instructions.

When the wine is clear, rack it into a clean demijohn and add a crushed Campden tablet or a teaspoonful (5 ml) of sulphite solution. If the wine is too dry for your taste, add sugar to taste and 1 teaspoonful (5 g) of potassium sorbate to the gallon (4.5 litres) to prevent the sweetening sugar from being fermented. A pound (450 g) of sugar boiled in ½ pint (280 ml) of water will provide a suitable syrup for adding to your wine little by little, until it reaches the desired sweetness.

The wine can then be bottled and stored in wine bottles. Use the mushroom-shaped stoppers if the bottles are to be stored upright and drunk soon, or long cylindrical corks if the wine is to be matured in a rack, or horizontally.

Dried Peach and Apricot

So early in the year, there are few fresh ingredients other than imported fruits, but there are some pleasant wines that can be made from dried fruits. Peaches and apricots can both be purchased dried and are eminently suitable for winemaking.

Both of these fruits may have been sterilised or bleached with sulphur dioxide as part of the drying process and, over the years, such dried fruits have become the home of certain sulphur-resistant bacteria. There is therefore little point in trying to sterilise them with Campden tablets or sulphite. Place the dried fruits of your choice in a bowl and sterilise and clean them with a kettleful of boiling water. Leave to soak for about 10 minutes, then drain and use in the following recipe.

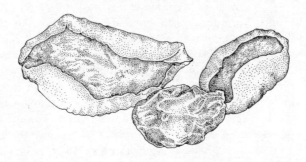

DRIED PEACH OR APRICOT WINE
1 lb (450 g) dried peaches or apricots
2¼ lb (1 kg) sugar
½ pint (280 ml) white grape concentrate
¼ teaspoon (1.5 g) tannin
2 teaspoons (10 g) pectic enzyme
1 teaspoon (5 g) nutrient
1½ teaspoons (7.5 g) tartaric acid
White wine yeast

Clean the fruit, as explained above, and cut it into small pieces. Drop it into 4 pints (2.3 litres) of boiling water, simmer for just 5 minutes, then remove the pan from the heat and leave the contents to soak overnight. Next day strain off the peaches or apricots and put them to one side. Pour the liquid into a clean bucket. Boil the sugar in 2 pints (1.1 litres) of water and allow to cool. Add it to the liquid and stir in all the other ingredients. Pour into a demijohn and fit a bung and airlock. Half fill the airlock with water and fit the dust-cap. The must should start fermenting within 48 hours if kept at about 70°F (21°C). After 2 weeks, top up to the shoulder of the jar with cold water and leave the demijohn until the fermentation ends. The wine should then clear naturally and all the sugar will have been used up by the yeast. Rack it off the sediment onto a crushed Campden tablet and sweeten to taste with sugar syrup. Add 1 teaspoonful (5 g) of potassium sorbate to the gallon (4.5 litres) to prevent the residual yeast cells from restarting the fermentation.

If the wine is slow to finish fermenting, you can rack it when it has reached a suitable level of sweetness, using a Campden tablet and a teaspoonful (5 g) of potassium sorbate. The wine may then have to be left to clear before bottling.

PEACH OR APRICOT JAM

3 lb (1.4 kg) sugar

Juice of 2 large lemons

Fruit discarded from previous recipe

This recipe is unusual in that the discarded fruit can be used again, to make a pleasant and economical jam.

Bring the sugar to the boil in 1 pint (560 ml) of water, together with the lemon juice. Stir constantly until the sugar is dissolved, then boil it for 5 minutes, stirring it continually. Add the fruit and boil for a further 15 minutes, continuing to stir it. It should by then have thickened and a small sample dripped onto a cold saucer should quickly start setting and the surface should wrinkle when prodded with a spoon. Pot in heated jam jars, and cover in the usual way. This makes 5 or 6 lb (2.3 or 2.7 kg) of jam.

As peaches and apricots are very high in pectin, this jam sets quite easily and you can experiment with using more or less sugar to taste, or substitute 2 teaspoonfuls (10 g) of citric acid if you have no lemons handy.

Prune

Another dried fruit that has a quite distinctive taste that can be put to good use is the prune. The extract from prunes is brown, with a flavour that blends in well with other fruits and juices to make a dessert-style wine similar in type to Marsala or sweet sherry.

PRUNE DESSERT WINE

1½ lb (680 g) prunes
1 lb (450 g) dates
1 lb (450 g) bananas
2½ lb (1.1 kg) sugar initially and 8 oz (225 g) added later
½ pint (280 ml) white grape concentrate (or 1 lb/450 g raisins)
1½ teaspoons (7.5 g) tartaric acid
1 teaspoon (5 g) pectic enzyme
1 teaspoon (5 g) nutrient
1 (3 mg) Vitamin B tablet
Wine yeast

Cut the prunes and dates into halves and put them into a sterile bucket. Peel the bananas, slice, and simmer in 2 pints (1.1 litres) of water for 15 minutes. Strain the hot liquor into the bucket and discard the banana pulp. Boil 2½ lb (1.1 kg) of sugar with 1½ pints (840 ml) of water and add that to the bucket while still hot. Pour in the grape concentrate, or minced raisins if preferred, the tartaric acid, nutrient and Vitamin B tablet and a further 2 pints (1.1 litres) of hot water. Stir well, cover, and leave to cool.

When the temperature has dropped to 75°F (24°C), add the pectic enzyme and the yeast, stir and cover again. Leave in the bucket for 5 or 6 days, stirring at least once a day. You will find that as the fermentation progresses the fruit will form a thick layer, or 'cap', at the surface, and this has to be broken up and mixed back into the must to get the maximum extract.

The next stage is to strain off the fruit, pouring the must into a demijohn. Do not press or squeeze the pulp to aid juice extraction or you will cause too much finely divided pulp to pass into the jar. Top the jar up with a further 8 oz (225 g) of sugar boiled in a ¼ pint of water (140 ml) and cooled. Fit a rubber bung and airlock, and leave to ferment for 2 weeks.

After a fortnight you will find a fairly thick sediment. Rack the wine off this, rinse the jar and return the wine to it, adding cold water so the wine barely reaches the shoulder of the demijohn.

Check the specific gravity after about 4 weeks and, when it drops to 1.000, add a further 4 oz (115 g) of sugar dissolved in a cup full of the wine, warmed in a saucepan. If the specific gravity drops again to 1.000, repeat the sugar addition.

The wine is finished when it clears, and should then be racked off the sediment onto a crushed Campden tablet or a teaspoonful (5 ml) of sulphite solution and a teaspoonful (5 g) of potassium sorbate. It can be sweetened to taste, usually to a specific gravity of at least 1.020, and the jar topped up with water. It may then be bottled and stored for a few months. If you can spare the demijohn, the wine is better left in the demijohn to mature. It is easy during this period to allow an airlock to dry out, and the jar is better sealed with a large cork bung. If the wine is matured in bulk, when it is eventually bottled it should rest for a few days before being drunk, to let it recover from the disturbance. This undoubtedly lets the wine give of its best.

On page 10, I explained the advantages of making up a standard sugar syrup by dissolving 2¼ lb (1 kg) of sugar in 1¹/₁₀ pints (625 ml) of water and using this syrup when cool.

In the preceding recipe, the sugar additions are simply made by adding ½ pint (280 ml) of syrup instead of boiling up 8 oz (225 g) or sugar, or ¼ pint (140 ml) instead of dissolving 4 oz (115 g). This method saves a lot of time and fiddling about and the bulk syrup can be kept in a screwtop jar or bottle until required. Future recipes will refer to sugar additions, but it is recommended that this is done in the form of cold sugar syrup, on the basis that 1 pint (560 ml) equals 1 lb (450 g) of sugar, and *pro rata*.

Coltsfoot

March and April bring the first flower of the year that can be used for making wine. Although it is a dainty little flower, the coltsfoot is a pernicious weed, difficult to eradicate and capable of driving its way through rock-hard ground, tarmac or virtually anything else that gets in its way. Obnoxious to the gardener, beloved of the herbalist, and welcomed by the winemaker, coltsfoot is a plant of great character. Despite everything, the bright little deep yellow flowers appear early in Spring, on the top of stalks wrapped in tiny leaves that look like scales. The coltsfoot is a perennial, rising on wastelands from an underground creeping rootstock. The flower is followed by the polygonal leaves, with the undersides covered in a white felt-like growth. Coltsfoot (*Tussilago farfara*) is a fragrant plant, named from the Latin word for cough, *tussis*, and has for centuries been used to soothe coughs and asthma in the dried form or taken as snuff, rolling the leaves like cigars, or more commonly using it as the base material for herbal tobacco.

Coltsfoot, as our first wildflower that is fermentable, is recognised for winemaking for its rich flavour; the only drawback is finding enough flower heads with which to make the wine.

COLTSFOOT WINE

3 – 4 pints (1.7 – 2.3 litres) coltsfoot flowers
2 ¼ lb (1 kg) sugar initially
½ pint (280 ml) white grape concentrate
1 teaspoon (5 g) tartaric acid
1 teaspoon (5 g) ammonium phosphate nutrient
1 (3 mg) Vitamin B tablet
¼ teaspoon (1.5 g) tannin
White wine yeast

Pour 4 pints (2.3 litres) of boiling water over the flower heads in a sterile bucket, then add 2 ¼ lb (1 kg) of sugar dissolved in just over 1 pint (600 ml) of water. Stir well and add the grape concentrate, tartaric acid, tannin and ammonium phosphate nutrient. Crush and add the Vitamin B tablet. When the mixture cools, add a white wine yeast, cover closely and stir daily for 7 days. Strain into a demijohn and add approximately 1 pint (560 ml) of water to bring the level of the must up to the shoulder of the jar. Fit a bung and airlock and leave to ferment until dry (SG 1.000 or less). Make up to a gallon (4.5 litres) with water, and stabilise with a teaspoonful (5 ml) of sulphite solution (or 1 Campden tablet) and a ¼ teaspoonful (1.5 g) of potassium sorbate. Sweeten to SG 1.005 – 1.010 and bottle.

Dandelion

Flowering next after the coltsfoot comes the glowing golden dandelion, another plant beloved of herbalists and food purists. Dandelions provide salad leaves (blanched with an upturned pot) and roasted roots to replace coffee, (I tried this and thought it better smoked in a pipe). Dandelions, as their French nickname *pissenlit* (pee-the-bed) warns you, have a reputation as a diuretic, but this need not deter the winemaker.

The great meadow pastures thick with wild flowers are now largely gone, due to modern herbicides that kill off all except the grasses for making hay or grazing. Dandelions are easily found along roadsides and the central reservations of trunk roads dual carriageways. These flowers gladden the eye, but are not only a hazard to pick, due to the traffic, but a hazard to health due to pollution. Motor vehicles deposit a constant haze of filth, composed of rubber dust, oil, diesel or petrol fumes, lead and various other toxic substances that coat everything for a few yards either side of the carriageway. Find a field or piece of waste ground, a country lane or a riverside bank to pick your dandelions and you will know they are unspoiled by road pollution and less likely to have been sprayed with weedkillers. Dandelions usually have a first flush of blooms in April and then flower spasmodically through the summer. In the United Kingdom, St George's Day, 23 April, is traditionally the day to pick dandelions and start off your wine.

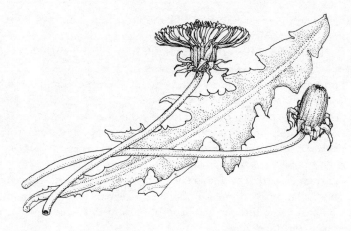

Dandelions produce a milky latex-like sap that has a bitter taste. The wine should therefore be made from the petals and as little greenery as possible if fresh flowers are used. Dried flowers are usually sold as whole heads, but the process of drying renders the sap innocuous. Use approximately 2 – 3 pints (1.1 – 1.7 litres) of petals or 4 – 6 oz (115-170 g) of dried flowers.

Do not fall into the trap of picking dandelion heads with the intention of removing the petals later. The flowers close up tightly and you will have a lot of difficulty removing the petals, and much wastage. Instead, hold the flower head in one hand and firmly wrench off the petals with the other. Your finger and thumb will turn black temporarily as the latex dries on them, but it's all worth while.

There are two distinct styles of dandelion wine. For a light-flavoured wine pour 4 pints (2.3 litres) of boiling water over the flowers, and continue as for the coltsfoot wine recipe above. Dandelions will also make a heavier fuller-bodied and stronger-flavoured social wine as described below.

DANDELION WINE

4 – 6 pints (2.3 – 3.4 litres) fresh dandelion flowers (or 6 – 8 oz/170 – 225 g of dried)

2¼ lb (1 kg) sugar initially

8 oz (225 g) minced raisins

1 orange

1 lemon

¼ teaspoon (1.5 g) tannin

1 teaspoon (5 g) nutrient

1 teaspoon (5 g) pectic enzyme

Wine yeast – Tokay or Bordeaux for preference.

Boil the dandelions in 4 pints (2.3 litres) of water for 15 minutes and pour the whole into a bucket. Add 2¼ lb (1 kg) of sugar as syrup, and the minced or chopped raisins, the zest (coloured skin) and juice of the orange and lemon, a ¼ teaspoonful

(1.5 g) of tannin and the yeast nutrient. Make up to about 7 pints (3.9 litres) with cold water and, when cool, add the pectic enzyme and an active wine yeast. Ferment in the bucket for 5 days, then strain off into a demijohn. Fit a bung and airlock, half-filled, and leave to ferment for 2 weeks.

There will probably then be a heavy sediment and the wine should be racked and then topped up to the shoulder of the jar with water.

Each time the wine's specific gravity drops to 1.000, or the wine tastes sugarless, add 4 oz (115 g) of sugar, or 5 fl oz (140 ml) of sugar syrup, until the fermentation slowly ends. You should then sweeten the wine to taste, if necessary, and stabilise it with sulphite and potassium sorbate. This should be a pleasantly sweet, but not sickly, social or semi-dessert wine with a fairly high alcohol content. It can be drunk shortly after, but will improve immeasurably if kept to mature for a few months.

Some winemakers use a little crushed root ginger in this wine, but for me this spoils the flavour of the dandelions.

You may have noticed that when raisins, or for that matter sultanas or currants, are specified, they are always to be minced or chopped. Whole dried grapes will blow up like little balloons in the fermenting bucket through taking up liquid, and the gases from fermentation within them. In consequence, unless you take the trouble to pop every one with a wooden spoon, or crush them with your fingers, you will end up discarding raisins that are bloated with valuable materials and that have contributed little to the wine. Breaking them up beforehand eliminates this wasteful practice, but it does mean your alcoholic blackbirds and thrushes on the compost heap stay sober longer.

Rhubarb

In April and early May the first rhubarb comes available and this has a delicate flavour, lacking the high acidity and coarseness of the heavier sticks that grow later in the summer.

RHUBARB WINE

3 lb (1.4 kg) rhubarb sticks
2¼ lb (1 kg) sugar as syrup
½ pint (280 ml) red or rosé grape concentrate
Wine yeast
¼ teaspoon (1.5 g) tannin
1 teaspoon (5 g) pectic enzyme

Cut up the rhubarb into small pieces, and soak it for 4 or 5 days in 4 pints (2.3 litres) of cold water with a Campden tablet or a teaspoonful (5 ml) of sulphite solution added, in a covered bucket. Strain into a demijohn and add all other ingredients. Fit a bung and half-filled airlock and leave to ferment. After 10 or 14

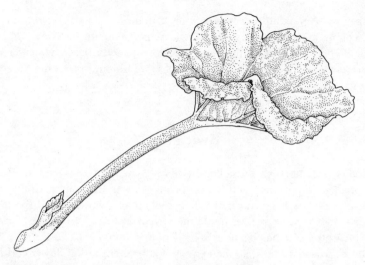

days, there may be a fairly heavy sediment and the wine should be racked and topped up to the shoulder of the demijohn with cold water.

When the fermentation ends, and the wine falls clear, rack again, adding a teaspoonful (5 ml) of sulphite solution and a teaspoonful (5 g) of potassium sorbate. The wine can then be slightly sweetened, and drunk chilled like a commercial rosé.

Gorse

About this time, gorse comes into bloom and, if you don't mind picking the flowers amidst prickles that will penetrate gloves, then pick 3 or 4 pints (1.7 or 2.3 litres) of the flowers and follow the coltsfoot wine recipe.

A word of warning: if you are a smoker, be extra careful with spent matches, cigarette ends etc. near gorse bushes. They will burn fiercely, the fire spreading with horrifying rapidity.

Remember when making any flower wine, the flowers as a rule add only their scent and colour and a little flavour to the wine. You must always add yeast nutrient, acid and some fruit or juice to give the wine body. Delicate flower wines; such as rose petal or elderflower, also need a small amount of tannin to give the wine interest.

Broom

Broom flowers are more easily collected than gorse, but they contain varying quantities of alkaloid poisons. As different people vary in their susceptibility to this wine's side-effects, I will say no more than that; if you wish to try broom wine, follow the coltsfoot wine recipe, using no more than 2 pints (1.1 litres) of flowers to the gallon (4.5 litres). It has been estimated that it would take 25 lb (11.5 kg) of broom plant to poison a horse, so the extract of a few handfuls of flowers diluted to make a gallon of wine is unlikely to have any deleterious effect on the homewinemaker. Although broom does contain very small quantities of cytosine, sparteine and scoparin, its dubious reputation is more likely to stem from the days when credulous peasants believed that scruffy old ladies could fly on their broomsticks. Which reminds me of the graffitum I once saw in a Lake District pub, commenting on a local brand of quite excellent beer: 'H . . . .y's, thee only way to fly!' Maybe broom wine has the same effect.

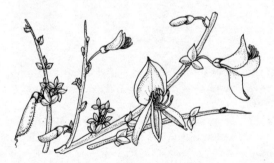

Brown Ale

Far more palatable in the early days of the year, when the weather can switch within hours from a warm sunny day to hail and frost, is a comforting sweet brown ale. This is a popular beer with a low hopping rate and probably the nearest of the modern drinks to the 'olden times' ales that were made before hops became used as the universal bittering and preservative ingredient. Brown ales are solid, satisfying drinks not too high in alcohol, with a sweet finish that the amateur achieves by adding a non-fermenting sugar. The following recipe is for 1 gallon (4.5 litres).

BROWN ALE

12 oz (340 g) dark malt syrup (or 10 oz/285 g of dried malt)
4 oz (115 g) brown sugar
1 oz (30 g) Fuggles hops
2 oz (60 g) crystal malt, coarsely crushed
Beer yeast – top fermenting

Simmer all the ingredients except the yeast in 4 pints (2.3 litres) of water for 20 minutes, then strain into a sterile bucket. Use a rigid sieve for the straining, as the hops and crystal malt husks will retain some of the sweet wort. The hops etc. can then be sparged, or rinsed through, with a spray of 2 pints (1.1 litres) of hot water to release the trapped sugars. Discard the hops and husks, which when cool will make a good mulch to go around your fruit bushes. Add 1½ pints (840 ml) of cold water and cover closely until the wort cools.

When the temperature drops to 21°C (70°F) 'pitch' the yeast or, in non-brewing parlance, sprinkle it over the top of the wort, and then replace the lid on the bucket.

By the next day, the fermentation should be under way and, a day or so later, the wort should be covered with a stiffish foam of froth and yeast. This should be skimmed off to prevent the surplus yeast spoiling the flavour of the beer. There may also be a brown 'tideline' at surface level, made up of yeast and harsh-flavoured hop resins. This too should be removed by wiping with a sterile cloth. Stir the beer well and replace the cover.

Repeat this on the following day and then rack the beer into a demijohn, with a teaspoonful (5 ml) of liquid beer finings stirred in. Fit a bung and airlock; beer is a low alcohol drink and needs protection. It is only during the first few days of heavy fermentation that the carbon dioxide produced protects the beer from airborne infections; thereafter the air should be excluded.

When the airlock shows that the fermentation has ended, by ceasing to pass through bubbles of carbon dioxide gas (usually about 5 to 7 days after the yeast is pitched) rack the beer off the sediment. Add 1½ fl oz (43 ml) of sugar syrup and 4 oz (115 g) of lactose sugar dissolved in a little hot water and make up to 1 gallon (4.5 litres) with cold water. The lactose is a non-fermenting sugar that will simply sweeten the beer, and the sugar syrup will cause a refermentation when the beer is bottled, giving the beer condition, i.e. a sparkle and liveliness from the carbon dioxide gas dissolved in it.

Bottle the beer in standard beer bottles, fitted with internal screw tops, with the rubber washers replaced where perished and thoroughly sterilised, or with crown caps. If you have no beer bottles, other containers designed to take a pressurised or carbonated beverage, such a lemonade bottles, can be used.

Label the beer clearly; there are many decorative labels on sale, but any label is better than none. Store the beer in the warm for 2 or 3 days for the bottle fermentation that will give the beer condition, then transfer it to a cool place for 2 or 3 weeks to mature.

Honey

One of the most ancient fermentable materials that today is available all the year round is honey. Honey is nectar collected by social bees (*Apis mellifera*) and stored in wax combs in the hive as a food reserve for the colony to live on in bad weather or in winter. The aroma and taste of honey vary with the type of flower from which the nectar has been collected and this does of course affect the wine, known as mead, that is made from honey.

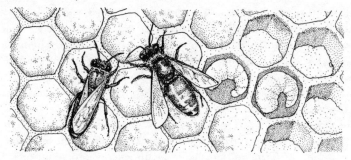

Beekeeping purists claim that mead should only be made from honey, water and mead yeast. Because of its low acid and nutrient content, mead made this way tends to ferment slowly and sluggishly for years. Most winemakers treat honey in a similar way to fruit juices or extracts, balancing the must, adding nutrient salts and using a true wine yeast. Such a yeast will ferment rapidly, produce more alcohol and settle more firmly than the powdery Maury yeast recommended for mead-making.

Because it is a liquid invert sugar, one and a fifth times as much honey is needed to replace the sugar that would usually be fermented in a wine. Although considerably more expensive than sugar, there is of course no extra cost of fruit or other ingredients needed to make mead, as the honey serves both purposes. It is immaterial whether you use clear or set honey for meadmaking, but be careful not to buy the invert-sugar spreads that are so much like set honey. The sugar will of course ferment perfectly well, but there will be neither a mead flavour nor bouquet in the finished product. For a pleasant sweet mead, try the following recipe for 1 gallon (4.5 litres).

MEAD

4 lb (1.8 kg) honey
½ oz (15 g) tartaric acid
½ teaspoon (2.5 g) grape tannin
1 teaspoon (5 g) nutrient
1 (3 mg) Vitamin B tablet
Wine yeast – Sherry or Tokay for preference

Put 4 pints (2.3 litres) of water in a pan and stir in 3 lbs (1.4 kg) or honey. Raise to simmering point, stirring frequently to prevent the honey from caramelising and, after 10 minutes, remove any froth and allow the contents of the pan to cool. Add the other ingredients and yeast, then make up to 7 pints (3.9 litres) with cold water.

Pour the must into a demijohn and fit a bung and airlock. When the mead must has fermented down to a specific gravity of 1.005 (almost dry) stir in 4 oz (115 g) of the remaining honey, allow to re-ferment, and repeat each time the specific gravity drops to 1.005 again. There will probably be sufficient honey to finally sweeten the mead when the fermentation has ended.

Rack the mead off the sediment, top up with water and stabilise it with sulphite and potassium sorbate. Store until you can resist it no longer, then sip and quietly savour this most delectable of drinks; it will take away the world's cares.

The reason for skimming the honey and water after simmering is to remove flower pollen, wax and other less welcome substances that may be in the honey. Honey does not ferment or suffer infections until diluted, as it has such a high sugar content. Once it is diluted with water there is a decided risk of spoilage from wild yeasts etc, and this too is why the mixture is heated. Boiling should be avoided as this drives off the distinctive flower fragrance that makes mead so enjoyable.

In Georgian and Victorian times, mead was very popular and honey was fermented with a variety of other ingredients. Our worthy ancestors most carefully identified these varied brews under particular names.

Cyser is honey fermented with apple juice (which alone would be cyder) and pyment is grape juice and honey. An easy introduction to pyment is to ferment a can of grape concentrate, such as a Mosel, substituting pale honey for the sugar that is usually required, finishing as a medium dry to medium sweet wine. Serve chilled, as with any light white wine.

All other fruits or fruit juices fermented with honey are known as melomel. High alcohol melomels should be sweet and served at room temperature, but others should be dry or only slightly sweet and served chilled. Strongly flavoured fruit, such as blackcurrants and elderberries, do not make very satisfactory light alcohol melomels because of their high tannin content. Spiced meads are popular, particularly where there is a high alcohol content. Most spices can be used, alone or in combination, and can best be added by infusing the spice in the mead or pyment, suspended in a piece of muslin or nylon cloth tied with a string. Using this method, the brew can be tasted at intervals, always a popular exercise, and the spices removed when the preferred depth of flavour has been reached. This variety of honey drink is known as hippocras.

Finally comes the blend of fermented honey with herbs and perhaps a little spice. This is believed to be a relic of the days when herbs were infused in alcohol to make medicinal drinks to be taken as a restorative or a cure for illness. Such drinks are known as metheglin, which is said to be a mediaeval Welsh term for medicine. That may only be a fancy, but it is a plausible one; the truth is that metheglin will do you good, as will any alcoholic drink, taken in moderate quantities.

Honey can of course be used as a substitute for sugar in any recipe, for mead, wine or even beer. It does have a very distinctive bouquet and flavour and this will be apparent in the finished product. If you like it, the comparatively small quantities used for the final sweetening of a wine will have a noticeable and pleasing effect.

Buttercups

May brings the early flowers that will ensure a rich harvest of fruit later in the year. Garden varieties of crab-apples and the usual dessert and cooking apples, cherries and plums, damsons and pears, all delight the eye with their blossom and the mind with pictures of bottles yet to come. Many other flowers appear in April and May such as the varied members of the buttercup family (Ranunculaceae), whose golden hordes are so pretty to see. Lesser celandines, marsh marigolds, and various buttercups, anemones and travellers' joy, all are related and all carry in the fresh plant an irritant poisonous yellow oil, proto-anemonin, which will cause vomiting, blistering and severe illness, possibly even death. The poison is rendered harmless by the plant being dried, which is why herbalists can sell lesser celandine, but, in my view, if the fresh plant is poisonous, then it is better avoided altogether.

Greater celandine, though of a different family, (Papaveraceae), was used in olden days for medicinal purposes. Culpeper, the famous seventeenth-century herbalist, recommended greater celandine for everything from cataracts on the eye to sores on the legs. Fortunately is it not prescribed nowadays, at least as a fresh plant material, so there are less victims of the four poisonous substances it contains.

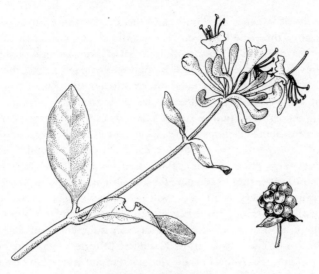

Honeysuckle

Honeysuckle now, with its sweetly scented clustered blooms, makes a delightful light flower wine. A word of warning, though; only the flowers are safe for winemaking. Honeysuckle produces heads of attractive berries, but they are poisonous. The following recipe should yield a light, delicate wine with a delicious bouquet.

HONEYSUCKLE FLOWER WINE

2 pints (1.1 litres) honeysuckle florets
2¼ lb (1 kg) sugar
½ pint (280 ml) white grape concentrate (or ½ lb/225 g minced sultanas)
1½ teaspoons (7.5 g) tartaric acid
1 teaspoon (5 g) nutrient
1 (3 mg) Vitamin B tablet
Pinch of magnesium sulphate (Epsom salts)
¼ teaspoon (1.5 g) tannin
White wine yeast

Rinse the honeysuckle florets in 2 pints (1.1 litres) of water with a crushed Campden tablet and strain without pressing, shaking lightly in a colander or sieve. Boil the sugar in 1½ pints (840 ml) of water and allow the syrup to cool. Put the flowers in a bucket, add the sugar syrup and all the other ingredients except the yeast, make up to 1 gallon (4.5 litres) with cold water and stir. Add the yeast and cover with the lid. Stir once or twice each day for 4 days, then strain and pour the must into a demijohn. Fit a bung and airlock and leave to ferment to dry.

This wine needs sweetening slightly and this can be achieved by adding a little more sugar, after the wine has been racked onto a teaspoonful (5 ml) of sulphite solution, and stirring in a teaspoonful (5 g) of potassium sorbate to prevent refermentation. Alternatively – and this applies of course to any wine that is being sweetened – a little sugar syrup can be stirred into a bottle of wine before serving it

A different appoach to this problem of sweetening without the yeast multiplying and restarting the fermentation, is to use a sweetener that the yeast cannot feed on. Glycerol, sold in chemists' shops as glycerine, is a natural constituent of wine and can be added to any wine that is dry or harsh. It tends to make the wine seem smoother, due to its effect on the palate, and does sweeten slightly. There are proprietary non-fermenting sweeteners for amateur winemakers on the market and these too are usually very good. You will occasionally come across references to sweetening with saccharine, but this synthetic material leaves a bitter aftertaste in the wine. There are now non-fermenting organic sweeteners on sale that are free from this after-taste, such as Searle's Canderel (Nutrasweet), and Hermes Gold tablets of Acesulfame K. A few of these dissolved in hot water can be added little by little until the wine suits your palate. It can then be safely bottled without any danger of re-fermentation gas blowing the corks and allowing air to bring spoilage organisms to the wine. The delicate flavour of the wine remains unaltered.

Mayflower

Mayflower blossom can be fermented – recipes are often listed under 'hawthorn'. This flower, for centuries the wedding flower for Greek brides, has a strange musky scent that is due in part, unromantically, to one of the chemical compounds also found in carrion. Despite this, may blossom will make a pleasing wine with an acceptable bouquet. Follow the honeysuckle wine recipe, using 3 pints (1.7 litres) of blossom and an extra 8 oz (225 g) of sugar.

Dried Elderberry and Rosehip Syrup

Strawberries are just coming in at the end of May but are far too expensive for winemaking. Instead, why not try a dry red table wine from this recipe? It can be made at any time of the year and is worth keeping for a few months to mature.

DRIED ELDERBERRY AND ROSEHIP WINE

6oz (170 g) dried elderberries (or 2 lb/900 g fresh or frozen)
12 oz (340 g) bottle of rosehip syrup
2 ¼ lb (1 kg) sugar
1 level teaspoon (4 g) ammonium phosphate
1 level teaspoon (4 g) tartaric acid
Juice and zest of 1 large or 2 small oranges
1 teaspoon (5 g) pectic enzyme
Bordeaux yeast

Place the elderberries in a pan with 2 pints of water (1.1 litres), bring to the boil and simmer gently for 10 minutes. Pour the contents of the pan into a sterile bucket and stir in the sugar until dissolved. Add other ingredients, except the yeast and pectic enzyme, and stir again. Top up to the gallon (4.5 litres) mark with cold water and, when the temperature has dropped to 24°C (75°F), add the yeast and pectic enzyme. Cover the bucket.

Ferment in the bucket for 5 or 6 days after the fermentation has started, stirring daily. Then strain the liquid into a demijohn and fit a bung and airlock. As the fermentation slows down, in say 2 weeks, rack and top up with cold water. Leave to ferment out to dry, add a teaspoonful (5 ml) of sulphite solution after racking, and leave to mature.

When making this wine, buy the least expensive rosehip syrup available. You are not buying it for its purity or suitability as a baby's dietary supplement, or to take advantage of its Vitamin C content. What is required is sufficient rosehip syrup to give the wine a little body (thickness) and slightly adjust the flavour and bouquet. You can in fact make your own syrup from wild rosehips in the Autumn and instructions will be found later in the book.

Dried elderberries are specified as anyone can buy these at any time of the year. Fresh elderberries are better, if in season, and frozen elderberries are as good as fresh.

Recipes of this type can be varied in many different ways, by adding a little grape concentrate, a few rose petals, the juice from a can of red fruit, or whatever you wish to try. One thing that surprisingly does not blend with elderberry is elderflower, but apart from that combination a fascinating range of slightly differing wines can be made with the same basic ingredients and small quantities of other materials as modifiers. One thing that must be stressed, keep detailed records of all the wines you make. One day you will produce a superb wine that you will want to repeat. Without such notes it will be impossible, for your memory will never supply all the information you want.

As a start, if you want to try a first variation on this wine, buy a tin of Cape loganberries and strain the juice into your demijohn. This will markedly alter the wine and you still have the fruit to use as a dessert.

Dried Elderflowers

Except perhaps in the most mild and protected parts of southern England, it is still too early, in May to expect the elder to be in full flower. So to give you a taste for this famous blossom, try this very simple recipe that makes a delicately fragrant sparkling wine, that can be made at any time of the year. It includes dried elderflowers, which are obtainable from most winemakers supply shops, herbalists, health food stores, and some chemists.

SPARKLING ELDERFLOWER WINE

1 oz (30 g) dried elderflower
1 lb (450 g) minced sultanas (or ½ pint/280 ml white grape concentrate)
1 ½ lb (675 g) granulated sugar
1 teaspoon (5 g) citric acid
1 teaspoon (5 g) pectic enzyme (or liquid equivalent)
Pinch of tannin powder
1 (3 mg) Vitamin B tablet
Champagne or Perlschaum yeast

Make a syrup of the sugar by bringing it to the boil with 1 pint (560 ml) of water. Put the dried elderflowers, acid, tannin and sultanas or concentrate in the bucket, pour on the hot syrup, stir well and cover. After half an hour, add 6 pints (3.4 litres) of cold water and then stir in the crushed Vitamin B tablet, pectic enzyme and yeast. Cover closely and stir daily for 3 days. Strain the liquid into a demijohn and fit the bung and airlock. Half-fill the airlock with water and a few drops of sulphite solution.

Leave the must to ferment until it has completely lost all sweetness. A sample that has been well stirred to disperse the dissolved gas, should register a specific gravity of 0.995 or less on the hydrometer.

Rack the wine, but do not add the usual crushed Campden tablet or teaspoonful (5 ml) of sulphite solution. Instead, stir in 1 oz (30 g) sugar, dissolved in a little hot water, then top the demijohn up to the neck with cold water and stir well – this is important.

As this is to be a sparkling wine, do take care to bottle it only in bottles made for the purpose, bottles designed to take tremendous internal pressure. Champagne or sparkling wine bottles must be used, free from any chips or scratches. Ordinary wine bottles may well burst under the gas pressure generated by the secondary fermentation that takes place in the bottle.

Syphon the wine into the bottles, leaving a space of about 3 inches (7.5 cm) measured from the top of the bottle. Cork with a plastic stopper and fasten the cork in place with wire. Very professional wire cages, or muselets, can be bought; these do the job perfectly and can be re-used over and over again, with just the occasional replacement of the piece of wire that goes round the neck of the bottle. Store these bottles upright and the yeast will stay in the punt of the bottle when the wine is poured 2 or 3 months later. Drink it slightly chilled – an hour in the refrigerator door should be enough. And do ease the stopper out of the bottle with a cloth in your hand. It will still make a pleasing pop! when withdrawn, but can't fly off and do any damage. Pour as much of the wine as possible without clouding into a glass jug, from which it can be poured as required into the wine glasses. Sparkling wines are best served in the tall champagne glasses known as 'flutes'. Except perhaps at party times, avoid those shallow saucer-like glasses usually sold as champagne glasses. Their lack of depth and large surface area allow the wine to lose its sparkle all too quickly.

Lager

Another sparkling beverage, to be made now, ready for the long hot days of summer when a long cool drink is welcome, is a clear pale lager. This can be made from one of the many kits on the market and, as with anything else, by and large you get what you pay for. Lager is such a light and delicate beer that it is well worthwhile buying the best you can. After all, if you make 5 gallons (22.5 litres) of lager for the approximate cost of 5 pints (2.8 litres) in a bar, then even the most expensive kit makes cheap lager. The same, of course, applies to kits for all types of beer.

Generally speaking, to make a good lager from separately purchased ingredients is only a little more trouble, and the lager can be adjusted slightly each time until it is exactly the way you like it – different varieties of hop, different strains of yeast, slight variations in the quantities of ingredients used, and the addition of small amounts of different grains, syrups etc. will all make noticeable differences in the final brew. It is strongly recommended that only one factor is altered at a time and that precise records are kept. Without these two precautions you might well find you almost have the brew of a lifetime and not know which factor made the difference, or you might actually make a superb batch of lager or other beer and be unable to repeat it. That would be a tragedy indeed! A straightforward basic lager recipe for 5 gallons (22.5 litres) is as follows:

LAGER

4 lb (1.8 kg) pale dried malt extract
2½ oz (75 g) Saaz or Hallertauer seedless hops
1 lb (450 g) white sugar
Lager yeast – bottom-fermenting

If you cannot buy good quality seedless Continental hops, buy the best Goldings hops you can and increase the quantity to 4 oz (115 g).

Boil the malt with the hops in a gallon (4.5 litres) of water for 20 minutes. If you haven't a big enough container, divide up the hops and the malt so both are in each batch you boil.

Pour through a strainer into a 5-gallon (22.5 litre) fermenting bin and rinse the hops with a kettleful of hot water. Slowly pour in the sugar, stirring continuously so it dissolves at once.

Add a further 3½ gallons (15.8 litres) of cold water and check the temperature is down to 75°F (24°C) or less. Pitch the yeast and cover closely.

This may not ferment as violently as the brown ale. Syphon it off into a 5-gallon (22.5 litre) fermenting vessel, or five 1 gallon (5 × 4.5 litre) demijohns, and protect under airlock until the yeast drops out, leaving a clear bright lager. Use finings according to the instructions if, improbably, the beer remains hazy for more than a few days after the airlock stops working.

Syphon the lager off the sediment and top it up with cold water to the full 5 gallons (22.5 litres). Run it into a keg, stirring in 4 oz (115 g) of sugar as syrup and fit the cap tightly; the lager should be drinkable in 10 to 14 days, though it will improve for several weeks. When you start using it, it is well worth fitting one of the patent caps that takes a small carbon dioxide bottle. These range from the soda-syphon bulbs upwards and maintain a protective layer of sterile gas over the beer as the level drops, preventing non-sterile air from being sucked in and bringing infections with it.

Alternatively, the lager can have the sugar syrup stirred thoroughly into the bulk and then it is ready for bottling. May I remind you again, the only safe bottles are those manufactured to contain fizzy drinks.

SUMMER

Roses

Among the first, and certainly the foremost of the summer flowers is that essential and fundamental part of the English garden, the rose. Though magnificent in their size, purity of colour and perfection of shape, many of the modern hybrids are sadly lacking in that one incomparable attribute of the rose, scent. As this is one of the main reasons for using rose petals in winemaking, it is well worth the winemaker's while to plant a few roses with his or her hobby in mind. Fragrant Cloud, Alec's Red and Ernest H. Morse are just three examples of roses with strong fragrance and they add beauty and colour to the garden as well. Some of the more deeply pigmented roses, such as Josephine Bruce, help heighten the colour of a pinkish wine; yellows, pinks and whites all blend down to a golden white wine.

Before you start to make rose petal wine, there are two things to remember. Firstly, you need to start off a fermentation of grape in some form – sultanas, bottled juice, canned grape concentrate – as rose petals are too insubstantial to make a wine on their own, unless excessive quantities are used; grape, nutrient and some acid are all needed initially. Secondly, as rose petals are so delicate they rapidly decompose, browning and breaking down within 2 or 3 days in the must. It is thus advisable to start a grape wine must fermenting before adding the petals. Allow the must to ferment for a couple of days and then immerse the rose petals in it. The alcohol already formed will help extract the perfume from the petals, which should be strained out after 2 or 3 days. This will avoid the deterioration in the petals being transferred to the wine and spoiling the flavour.

When collecting the petals, take bright young blooms, not the tired old things that are ready to shed petals and earwigs all over the garden. Take them when the dew is off them and before the day gets too hot and dry for the scent to be released.

Rose petals can be gently dried in the sun, if you cannot use them straight away or, of you have a deep freeze chest, they will keep even better if packed in polythene bags and frozen. The following recipe will give 1 gallon (4.5 litres) of a medium, delicate rosé wine.

ROSE PETAL WINE

2 pints (1.1 litres) rose petals, lightly pressed
13 fl oz (365 ml) white or rosé grape concentrate (this is half a standard 2 ¼ lb/1 kg tin
OR 1 lb/450 g minced sultanas)
2 ¼ lb (1 kg) granulated sugar as syrup
1 teaspoon (5 g) tartaric acid
1 teaspoon (5 g) nutrient
5 pints (2.8 litres water)
Wine yeast – perhaps a Sherry

Start the bucket fermentation going with all the ingredients except for the petals. Two days later, pick the petals and rinse them gently in a weak sulphite solution to banish the assorted visible and invisible livestock that is bound to accompany them. Drain and shake the petals lightly, then stir them into the fermenting must. After another 2 days, sieve the must and put the liquid into a demijohn. Top up to the shoulder of the jar with water and fit a bung and half-filled airlock.

Leave in a warm place to ferment out, then rack and stir in a crushed Campden or a teaspoonful (5 ml) of sulphite solution. Sweeten to taste with sugar syrup and a teaspoonful (5 g) of potassium sorbate, or with a non-fermenting sweetener, and bottle. This wine is best drunk as medium dry.

Rose petals are of course a perfect material to use to enhance the bouquet of another wine that lacks a good natural aroma from its ingredients. 2 or 3 oz (60 – 85 g) should be enough for most wines and they should be removed after 2 days in the fermentation.

Grape Vine

With the sudden surge in growth at this time of year, any owner of a grape vine, indoor or outdoor, will be blessed with a surfeit of soft, sappy young growth that has to be pruned back. This waste material is full of nutrients and sugary sap and can be used as the main ingredient in some surprisingly good wines.

Use the soft young growth that would otherwise shade and starve the infant grapes, which should be well set and growing; tendrils, leaves, stems, all young growth can be used. Do not use the ripened, hard old twigs and branches as these will give the wine rather a harsh flavour. You may also severely damage the vine, as ripe wood heals very slowly when cut. Unless the hardwood pruning is done in

winter, when the sap is down and the dormant vine has a chance to form a callus over the wound, it will bleed sap heavily from every cut. If your vine should suffer this way in error, the old-fashioned cure, which does work, is to force the cut ends into pieces of raw potato. One of my vines was once so ill-treated in my absence and I returned home to what looked like a french-fried chip tree in the greenhouse. It survived.

The French for leaf being *feuille*, this was quickly anglicised into 'folly', and this type of foliage wine has been known as Folly ever since. It is reminiscent of a light, medium sherry.

FOLLY

4 lb (1.8 kg) vine prunings – approximately
3 lb (1.4 kg) sugar
1 teaspoon (5 g) pectic enzyme
1 teaspoon (5 g) citric acid
1 (3 mg) Vitamin B tablet
Tokay wine yeast

Twist and bundle the vegetation with your hands, bruise with a heavy wooden mallet or rolling pin, and place in a bucket. Pour over it 4 pints (2.3 litres) of boiling water. Cover, and leave for 48 hours, then strain into a demijohn and add the pectic enzyme and yeast. Add the sugar (when cool after boiling 2 lb (900 g) in 1 pint (560 ml) of water) and the crushed Vitamin B tablet, nutrient and acid, stirring vigorously. Top up with water if necessary, to the bottom of the shoulder and fit a rubber bung and airlock.

When the wine has fermented for about 2 weeks, the rate of fermentation should drop and the specific gravity should be below 1.010. If it is not, leave it for another week. Add the other 1 lb (450 g) of sugar boiled in ½ pint (280 ml) of water and, when it has cooled, stir it well into the demijohn, topping up as necessary with cold water. Refit bung and airlock.

When the sweetness has dropped to the level that suits your palate it can be stabilised by racking and adding a teaspoonful (5 ml) each of sulphite solution and potassium sorbate. May I remind you that when stabilising a wine with unfermented sugar as the sweetener both chemicals must be used. Fining may be needed.

Alternatively, and preferably, the wine can be left to ferment for as long as it will, thus increasing the alcohol content. It should then be stabilised and sweetened to taste after it has fallen clear and been racked.

The demijohn should be topped up with water and the neck securely plugged with a hard plug of dry unmedicated cotton wool. Be most careful to change the plug if it gets wine splashed on it. Store the wine in the cool for a month or two, giving time for the filtered air to percolate slowly through the cotton wool and allowing the wine to oxidise slightly. This tends to produce aldehydes which will make your wine more sherry-like. However, regular tasting is advised, to make sure that the wine does not become over-oxidised and its bouquet and flavour spoilt. Rack and bottle finally.

Redcurrants

One of the early bush fruits from the garden is the redcurrant. This, like the white currant, fruits on the spurs of old wood and not on the young wood as does its cousin the blackcurrant.

Redcurrants are high in citric acid, plus a little malic acid, and are roughly half as acid as pure lemon juice. Because of this the fruit content of your wine need only be, say 2 lb (900 g) of redcurrants, and perhaps some banana to give the wine some body. Grape concentrate should not be used, if possible, as this will increase the acid content. If you are really keen to use a lot of fruit, then the acid can be reduced by adding sodium bicarbonate or calcium carbonate (i.e. powdered chalk), say 1 heaped teaspoonful (6 g) for each extra 1 lb (450 g) of fruit. Some frothing will follow, quite violently in the case of the sodium bicarbonate, and you should make sure there is room for it in the bucket. There is always a danger of the flavour being affected and I find it preferable to restrict the redcurrants instead.

REDCURRANT WINE – TAVEL-TYPE ROSÉ

2 – 2½ lb (0.9 – 1.1 kg) fresh redcurrants
1 lb (450 g) bananas
2¼ lb (1 kg) sugar
1 (3 mg) Vitamin B tablet
Pectic enzyme
Wine yeast

First of all, pour two pints (1.1 litres) of boiling water over the redcurrants and leave them to soak in the bucket. Peel the bananas, discarding the skins, and cut the fruit into ½ inch (13 mm) chunks. Put them in a pan with 2 pints (1.1 litres) of water, bring it to the boil and then simmer gently for 15 minutes. Remove from the heat, strain off the liquid and put it to one side to cool. The solids from the bananas can be discarded.

When the redcurrants have cooled, they should be mashed at least sufficiently to break their skins and the pectic enzyme added. Pour in the cooled banana liquor and the sugar in the form of sugar syrup. Add the Vitamin B tablet, crushed, and the wine yeast. Stir well and cover.

Stir daily for 5 days, the strain out the solids and put the fermenting must in a demijohn. Rack after 10 days and top up to the shoulder if necessary with cold water. Refit the bung and airlock and leave the wine to ferment to dry.

If preferred, this wine can be sweetened slightly after racking and stabilising. Try it on a hot summer's day, with a sprig of lemon thyme or borage, ice and lemonade, as a cooling long drink.

Gooseberries

Gooseberries have so long been a part of the English diet – since at least the fifteenth century – that they have found their way into the phrase 'playing gooseberry', meaning to be an unwanted chaperone, and inquisitive children have long been told their origin was 'under a gooseberry bush'. Gooseberries are invaluable in more tangible ways, too, as they are high in pectin and thus make jam with the least possible difficulty, needing only to be cooked gently until the skins soften and then boiled smartly with sugar for a few minutes. Use the ratio of 3 parts of fruit to 4 parts of sugar. When the jam reaches setting point – drip a little onto a cold dry saucer and let it cool; the surface will wrinkle when prodded if setting point has been reached – ladle it into preheated jam jars, and seal with waxed discs and proprietary jam pot covers. Stewed gooseberries make a pleasing dessert and as gooseberry fool – blended with cream – are food for the gods, with gooseberry pie a close second.

But despite their high acid and pectin content, gooseberries are greatly valued for winemaking. The first early green little gooseberries make a fine hock-type wine, giving a pale white beverage with the crisp fruity tang of malic acid that typifies many German wines.

GOOSEBERRY HOCK

2¼ lb (1 kg) fresh gooseberries – approximately
2¼ lb (1 kg) sugar as syrup
½ lb (450 g) chopped or minced raisins (or ½ pint/280 ml white grape concentrate)
1 (3 mg) vitamin B tablet
1 teaspoon (5 g) nutrient
1 teaspoon (5 g) pectic enzyme
Wine yeast

Rinse the gooseberries in sulphited water, then drain and roughly crush them. This is made easier by pouring a kettleful of boiling water over them first. Add the sugar syrup, allow to cool, and then add the other ingredients. Ferment for 5 days,

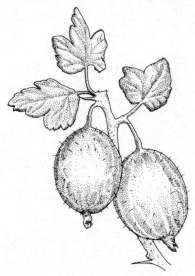

stirring once or twice each day to break up the 'cap', or surface layer of fruit, to obtain a better extract. Keep covered in between stirrings.

After 5 days, strain, without using any pressure on the pulp, into a démijohn. The pulp can be rinsed through with a little water and this is strained off and used to top up the level in the demijohn. Rack 2 weeks later and make up to a full gallon (4.5 litres). Leave to ferment to dry, then rack and sulphite.

Unsulphited gooseberries, being high in malic acid, are particularly prone to lactic acid bacteria which convert malic acid to lactic acid, which has a much less sharp flavour, and carbon dioxide gas. This malo-lactic fermentation, as it is known, improves the flavour of an over-acid wine and gives it a pleasant sparkle at the same time. Of course the corks may blow and, if this is not noticed and remedied, the wine will quickly spoil. Malo-lactic fermentations are probably the reasons behind the old belief that gooseberry wine started 'working' again in the Spring of the following year.

Gooseberries can often be bought quite cheaply, in A10 cans – catering packs containing 6 – 7 lb (2.8 – 3.3 kg) of fruit and juice. One of these, a 2 ¼ lb (1 kg) can of white grape concentrate, and 11 lb (5 kg) of sugar, will make 5 gallons (22.5 litres) of light table wine. Add 5 teaspoonfuls (25 g) of nutrient, five (15 mg) crushed Vitamin B tablets, and a couple of hefty doses, 6 teaspoonfuls (30 g), of pectic enzyme. A little extra acid, say 4 teaspoonfuls (20 g) of citric, and a ½ teaspoonful (2.5 g) of tannin powder will improve the brew. Make it in the same way as the preceding 1 gallon (4.5 litre) recipe.

Herbs

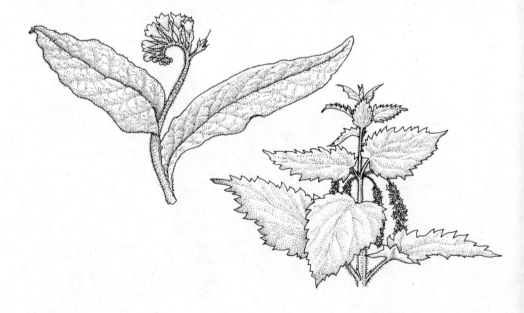

Wine can be made from many different ingredients and recipes have been published for many weird materials, such as onions and Christmas cake. But there are many less bizarre ingredients with a long history behind them of use for winemaking, quite possibly stemming from original herbal concoctions produced for medicinal reasons. Comfrey, nettle and lemon thyme are typical of this group and make wines of unusual flavours that are not always readily acceptable.

Parsley

A distinctly good plant for winemaking is parsley, which is easily grown from seed, purchased as a plant or bought from a greengrocer ready for use. This will make quite a pleasant wine.

PARSLEY WINE
¾ – 1 lb (340 – 450 g) fresh parsley
½ pint (280 ml) white grape concentrate (or 1 lb/450 g minced or chopped sultanas)
2¼ lb (1 kg) sugar
Juice and zest of 2 lemons
1 teaspoon (5 g) nutrient
Wine yeast

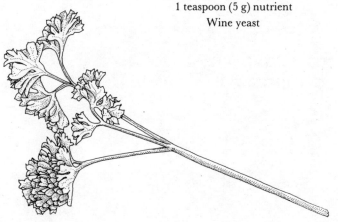

Chop the parsley coarsely and bring to the boil in 2 pints (1.1 litres) of water. Simmer for 20 minutes, then strain the liquid into a sterile bucket. Add the sugar and stir well until dissolved. Pour in 4 pints (2.3 litres) of cold water and add the sultanas or grape concentrate and the juice and zest of the lemons. The zest is the thin coloured surface layer of the peel. Hold each lemon over the bucket while removing the zest, as the skin is charged with volatile oils that are full of scent and flavour which will otherwise be lost. Add the nutrient and stir well. When cool, put in the yeast and cover.

Strain off after 4 or 5 days and put under airlock. Leave undisturbed until the fermentation has ended, then rack onto a teaspoonful (5 ml) of sulphite solution, or a crushed Campden tablet, and make up to a full gallon (4.5 litres) with water.

This is undoubtedly the best way of using parsley, as its harsh iron flavour is well diluted. Sweeten the wine if preferred using a non-fermenting sweetener (such as Acesulfame K or Searle's Nutrasweet) or a little sugar dissolved in some of the wine warmed in a pan. If sugar is used, stir a teaspoonful (5 g) of potassium sorbate into the demijohn to prevent refermentation.

Rumtopf

Of course, there are other ways of utilising fruit besides making wine and jam, or freezing it. One unusual method is by means of a rumtopf, a German way of producing both a delicious liqueur-like drink and a rich fruit compôte with many uses as a dessert etc. A rumtopf is a wide-mouthed ceramic jar with a lid, capable of holding several pounds of fruit and sugar and a bottle or two of rum. Many ancient pots have a soft glaze containing lead, which is alcohol-soluble and poisonous, so ensure that your rumpot is modern and with a hard glaze.

Unglazed pots will absorb alcohol and it will evaporate from the surface, which is a terrible waste of expensive spirit. Brandy producers lose alcohol by evaporation from the oaken barrels they use, and refer to this as 'the angels' share'. In this instance, don't side with the angels, keep the spirits firmly inside the jar.

The basic idea of a rumtopf is that, as the seasons pass, whatever fruit becomes available is soaked in half its weight in sugar for about an hour and then tipped into the rumtopf. Rum is then poured in until the fruit is covered and the lid is then replaced. Some fruit will float and this can be overcome, if you think it necessary, by placing a saucer or small plate on top of the fruit, removing and replacing it as new fruit is added.

When buying rum for your rumtopf, choose the dark rum, usually sold as Navy rum, in preference to white rum such as Bacardi. Occasionally, due to the dilution of the rum by the juice within the fruit, fermentation will start. This does not spoil the rumtopf, except if by mischance the wild yeast is an ill-flavoured one, but it is somewhat disconcerting to have a rumtopf burping large bubbles of gas at you. This can be avoided by buying rum with an alcohol content of over 40% (the old-style 70° proof); it is not always readily available, but is worth asking for.

Some fruits are not really suited to making rumtopf; blackcurrants are very acid and their skins become tough and chewy. Recommended are strawberries, cherries (don't bother to remove the stones), peaches, apricots, pears, plums, pineapples and, occasionally, a handful of blackberries or dewberries to heighten the colour. The larger fruits should be stoned or cored. Apples too can be included, but cut them fairly small and restrict the amount. Citrus fruits generally are not recommended, but if you have any surplus tinned fruits they can be added. The list of fruits is endless, but among the more obvious are grapes, melons and bananas.

All that is required is that you keep adding to the rumtopf fruit soaked in half its weight in sugar, cover it with strong dark rum, and keep the lid on. From October, the rumtopf can just be left to mature quietly until December. You will then have a jar full of rich fruit and a sweet liquor, that can be eaten and drunk either together or separately. The fruit can be used in flans, eaten with cream or ice cream, as part of a trifle, and in many other ways. There is no waste; any surplus that remains after Christmas can be used as the base of the rumtopf for the coming year.

So, as soon as the first strawberries appear, start your rumtopf. You can of course, refer to it just as a rumpot, but it doesn't sound quite as attractive then. If you don't have a rumtopf jar to use, then you can use any suitable container; a cheap substitute is a large sweet-jar, but this needs a cover to shut out the light – self-adhesive vinyl will suffice – and it won't be elegant enough to grace your Christmas sideboard. But you would have a rumtopf to enjoy.

Strawberries

With the coming of Summer everyone – except those unfortunate souls with an allergy to them – looks forward to the first strawberries. And those expensive

morsels only whet one's appetite for the heavy crops that follow. If you have a wholesale market in your area, this is the cheapest place to buy any type of fruit and with strawberries it is sometimes cheaper to buy them wholesale than it is to visit a pick-your-own farm. Regardless of the source, strawberries are superb and, as well as making magnificent jam, delicious flans and dozens of other fruit and cream desserts, they are an excellent fruit for winemaking. Strawberries are best used for sweet wines, as they have a sweet taste and aroma that do not suit the drier types of wine. They are also surprisingly high in citric acid, the amount varying with the season and variety. Strawberries are also high in tannins, equal to the heavily pigmented blackcurrants and, as any jam-maker can tell you, have a good pectin content too, about 0.5%, which is a fairly average figure for fresh fruit.

STRAWBERRY WINE
3 lb (1.4 kg) fresh or frozen strawberries
3 lb (1.4 kg) sugar
2 teaspoons (10 g) pectic enzyme
1 teaspoon (5 g) nutrient
Burgundy yeast

Thaw the fruit, if frozen, or rinse with weak sulphite solution and drain if fresh, and then pulp it with a potato-masher, a liquidiser or a bottle full of water. Make sure your bucket is stood on a thick pad of old newspapers to cushion the shock and save it from splitting. Boil 2 lb (900 g) of sugar in 2 pints (1.1 litres) of water and pour it onto the strawberry pulp when cool. Add a further 4 pints (2.3 litres) of water, the pectic enzyme, the nutrient salts and the yeast, and ferment on the pulp for a week. Strain into a demijohn, and rack off the sediment after 2 weeks. Top up to the shoulder with water.

When the wine tastes dry (SG about 1.000), add 8 oz (225 g) more sugar as syrup. Repeat this when the wine tastes dry again and leave until the fermentation ends and the wine is clear.

Rack again onto a crushed Campden tablet or a teaspoonful (5 ml) of sulphite solution, and sweeten further to taste. Stabilise with a teaspoonful (5 g) of potassium sorbate.

This makes a rich fruity wine, which, some people have suggested, would go well poured over ice cream. Don't waste it on such vandals!

Fresh strawberries can be hulled, rinsed with sulphite and drained. Dredged with sugar and frozen as separate fruits, they are just about acceptable for decorating tarts and flans. No matter how carefully you freeze and thaw them, they will always finish up rather flabby in texture. For winemaking supplies, don't bother with the sugar, just freeze them in bulk after cleaning and when they thaw they will be nice and soggy, ready for pulping.

While on the subject of deep-freezing fruit, the usual texts and handbooks tell you to freeze the fruit as quickly as possible, so that only small ice crystals form within and the fruit is not damaged. Winemakers, however, want the highest possible extract from the fruit with the least possible effort, so the best way is to ignore the cabinet's fast-freeze compartment and just let the fruit freeze slowly in the bulk part of the cabinet. The cells in the fruit will be ruptured by the larger ice crystals that form in them and the fruit, when thawed, will be soft and easily pulped. The juice will run beautifully freely, especially if you can put the fruit through a wine press, and the period of frozen storage also helps to reduce the pectin content slightly. Remember, a full freezer is cheaper to run than a half-empty one, so as the seasons change, fill up with whatever fruit becomes cheap and plentiful.

Blackcurrants

Blackcurrants, by comparison, are high in acid, mainly citric, very strongly flavoured and twice as high in pectin. The best use for them is to make blackcurrant jam, with pies a close second. For winemaking, blackcurrants are best used as a minor ingredient in a mixed fruit wine and, unless you wish the blackcurrant nose and flavour to be predominate, or even be clearly identifiable, restrict the fruit content to 8 oz (225 g) per gallon (4.5 litres).

There are many blackcurrant recipes published, based on bottled juices and syrups. However, it has been a common source of complaint that these musts will not ferment well, leaving the winemaker with a stickily sweet brew fit only for blending. It was long thought that blackcurrant syrups contained a preservative that was bad for the yeast, but later work has suggested that the yeast is inhibited by the fruit's high Vitamin C content. It would not be fair to recommend a recipe that might well produce little more than a cough cure, so here is a recipe that has successfully resulted in a strongly flavoured fruity wine.

BLACKCURRANT AND REDCURRANT WINE

1 lb (450 g) fresh or frozen blackcurrants
¾ lb (340 g) fresh or frozen redcurrants
2½ lb (1.1 kg) sugar
13 fl oz (365 ml) red grape concentrate (half a standard can)
1 teaspoon (5 g) nutrient
1½ teaspoons (7.5 g) pectic enzyme
1 teaspoon (5 g) Bentonite powder
Tokay or vigorous wine yeast

Pulp the fruit; convert the sugar to syrup and pour it while still hot, over the fruit. Add 4 pints (2.3 litres) of water and stir. When cool, add all the other ingredients except the grape concentrate. Ignore the instructions on the Bentonite package, just add the powder to the demijohn. It will work perfectly satisfactorily, combining with protein during the fermentation, leaving a clear wine at the end.

Ferment on the pulp for 4 or 5 days, strain the must into a demijohn and fit an airlock. Two weeks later, rack the young wine off the sediment and add the grape concentrate. Refit the airlock and continue the fermentation. When it has come to an end, rack again onto a Campden tablet or teaspoonful (5 ml) of sulphite solution and taste. The wine will be harsh-flavoured, but ignore this and concentrate on its degree of sweetness. Stabilise the wine with a teaspoonful (5 g) of potassium sorbate and sweeten to taste. This is a wine that should be kept for a few months to mature, during which period it will mellow in flavour and smooth off in texture. If still a little harsh to your palate, add a small quantity of glycerine, say 1 teaspoonful (5 ml) to the bottle, and mix well. This does not alter the wine, but it will delude your palate slightly. There are also quick-maturing preparations on the market, which are intended to make a rough young wine more acceptable and one of these might be found helpful.

If, despite your love of blackcurrants, you find the flavour or bouquet of even this wine a little too strong, do not try to alter it by dilution or flavourings. Save it for blending with wines of lesser quality, wines that are a bit thin or of indifferent flavour. Everybody makes one at sometime.

Raspberries

July brings the raspberry (*Rubus idaeus*), a delicious fruit that is familiar to everyone. A native wild fruit, the raspberry grows freely in clearings or on the edges of woodland, liking damp shady locations. Wild raspberries are smaller and pippier than the garden varieties, but have a superb flavour. Garden raspberries, too, like plenty of moisture and rich humus and grow freely, producing new canes each year that will bear the following year's crop; old cane should be cut out annually.

Raspberries hybridise freely with other members of the *Rubus* group and, as there are several species of raspberry, and many species of blackberry, the number of possible hybrids and reselections is almost infinite. Some have a short life of popularity, others go on endlessly. Where now will you find a King's Acre berry, or a phenomenalberry? How many gardeners own a mahdiberry, or have even heard of one? By comparison, the loganberry, said to be a natural sport or hybrid that grew in the garden of a Judge Logan in California, has been grown in the United Kingdom since 1897. The loganberry is so well established as a plant that some authorities grant it a name of its own as a recognised species, *Rubus loganbaccus*. Other well-known hybrids include the thornless boysenberry, with its rich purple-

red fruits, and the most recent addition, the tayberry from Scotland, bearing long purple berries with a delicious flavour.

All these raspberry relatives share a common factor with the true raspberry and that is a distinct and strong fruity flavour, usually accompanied by a sweet, matching aroma. Although raspberries are a magnificent fruit, probably second only to the strawberry in flavour and scent, they are so strong that a wine made from too many raspberries tends to finish up tasting rather like children's boiled sweets, or chemist's linctus. Generally, the flavour of raspberries is more suited to sweet wine than dry and, even in sweet wines, the fruit will dominate all else unless the amount used is restricted. This also applies to the hybrids, but to a lesser extent; a 14¼ oz (515 g) can of loganberries added to a port-style recipe (see page 112) will give the wine some of the fruitiness that is found in a commercial port.

Many people, however, enjoy the distinctive and rich flavour and smell of raspberries, so here is a simple recipe you can try. It is equally suitable for any of the hybrid fruits. If you don't have sufficient raspberries, tayberries or whatever your chosen fruit is, supplement what fruit you have by adding fresh apple or grape juice, the ready-to-drink type sold in cardboard litre packs. Use approximately 1 pint (560 ml) of juice to replace 1 pound (450 g) of fruit. This will keep the wine full-bodied, without spoiling the flavour of the chosen fruit.

SWEET RASPBERRY WINE

3 lb (1.4 kg) fresh raspberries
1 pint (560 ml) grape concentrate (or 1½ lb/675 g raisins)
3¼ lb (1.5 kg) sugar
1 teaspoon (5 g) nutrient
1 teaspoon (5 g) pectic enzyme
1 teaspoon (5 g) Bentonite powder
Wine yeast

Rinse the raspberries with a crushed Campden tablet, or a teaspoonful (5 g) of sulphite solution, in a pint (560 ml) of water, and drain. This is important with raspberries as they are a fragile fruit and the slightest damage can lead to wild yeast and bacterial infection, and the next step from that is acetic acid – vinegar! Raspberry wine vinegar would be a decided asset to the cookery enthusiast, but not by the gallon!

Crush the fruit and place it in a bucket with the grape concentrate or raisins. The grape concentrate can be white or red, though the red is preferable.

Dissolve 2¼ lb (1 kg) of sugar in 1½ pints (840 ml) of boiling water, cool, and pour over the fruit. Add 4 pints (2.3 litres) of cold water and the rest of the ingredients and the yeast. Ferment on the pulp for 5 days, then strain into a demijohn and continue the fermentation under airlock.

Rack after a fortnight and return the fermenting must to the clean demijohn. Don't top up with water as the space is needed for extra sugar.

When the fermentation slows down (SG 1.005 or less), warm a little of the wine in a pan and dissolve 8 oz (225 g) of sugar in it. When it has cooled, return it to the demijohn. This added sugar should ferment away, and the process can be repeated with a further 4 oz (115 g) of sugar at intervals until the fermentation ends and you are left with a clear, delectable sweet raspberry wine. Rack onto a crushed Campden tablet or a teaspoonful (5 ml) of sulphite solution and stabilise the wine with a teaspoonful (5 g) of potassium sorbate.

This wine will both smell and taste of raspberries, a real summer beverage, and if you wish to add a touch of Continental elegance you can label it 'Grand Vin de Framboises'.

Another attractive and distinct species of Rubus not uncommonly found in gardens is R. phoenicolasius, the Japanese wineberry, which is usually grown as a decorative perennial in flower beds, noted in particular for the fine red-bristly stems and orange fruit that ripens in August. Although grown as an ornamental, it is well worth growing for its berries.

Raspberries, boysenberries and the rest of the clan are eminently suitable for inclusion in your rumtopf. Take 1 lb (450 g) of fruit, or as near to it as you have,

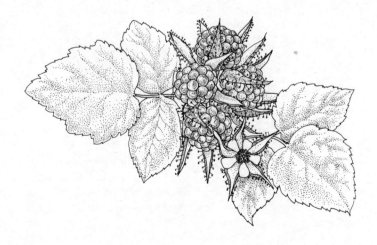

and soak it in 8 oz (225 g) of sugar for an hour or so, then add it to your rumtopf. Cover with rum and replace the lid.

Flower Wines

During July and August there are many flowers that can be used for winemaking. These include such diverse old favourites as rose petal, marigold and golden rod. For most of these use either the delicate honeysuckle wine recipe on p. 63 or the slightly more robust dandelion or rose petal wine recipes (pp. 55 and 71 respectively), according to the strength of colour and bouquet of the flower concerned. Golden rod is strongly flavoured and for most people 1 pint (560 ml) of

flowers is sufficient. Meadowsweet blossom should be fermented quickly after picking, as should most flowers, as they tend to deteriorate soon after harvesting. For most flowers a loosely-pressed 4 pints (2.3 litres) of fresh blossom is ample, but the flowers must be supported by grape concentrate or juice, or raisins or sultanas.

Salad Burnet

In the north of England grows the greater salad burnet (*Poterium sanguisorba officinalis*), a tall, spindly plant whose slender stalks are topped with purple-lilac florets growing from densely packed red-brown heads. These heads are picked before the flowers are fully opened and can be used to make one of the deepest red and most strongly flavoured wines possible from a British wild flower. Burnet wine has a distinctive, slightly powdery flavour, which is quite enjoyable and goes well with the deep purple-red colour. The Burnet grows wild along damp ditch edges, roadside wastes and pastures, and can be picked from July onwards. It can be made, as an exception to the rule, without grape, though ½ pint (280 ml) of concentrate instead of 8 oz (225 g) sugar will improve the wine slightly.

BURNET WINE – MEDIUM SWEET

4 pints (2.3 litres) burnet heads
2 ¾ lb (1.2 kg) sugar
1 ½ teaspoons (7.5 g) citric acid
1 teaspoon (5 g) nutrient
1 (3 mg) Vitamin B tablet
Wine yeast

Bring the flower heads to the boil in 2 pints (1.1 litres) of water, and simmer gently for 20 minutes. Let stand for 5 minutes, then pour the strained liquor over the rest of the ingredients (except yeast) and stir well. Add 4 pints (2.3 litres) of water and, when cool, the yeast. Transfer to a demijohn and ferment under airlock. Rack and sulphite when finished. If this wine ferments out to dry (below SG 1.000), sweeten to taste and stabilise with potassium sorbate.

Apricots

About this time of year, fresh apricots and peaches appear in the shops and on market stalls. Apricots are probably as cheap in July as at any time and can be used to make another sweet and enjoyable wine.

APRICOT DESSERT WINE

4 lb (1.8 kg) fresh apricots
2 lb (900 g) bananas
3 ½ lb (1.6 kg) sugar – approximately
2 teaspoons (10 g) pectic enzyme
1 teaspoon (5 g) nutrient
¼ teaspoon (1.5 g) tannin
Wine yeast

Boil 2 ¼ lb (1 kg) sugar in 2 pints (1.1 litres) of water and pour it over the apricots to soften them. Leave for an hour, then pulp the fruit, removing as many stones as possible. In the meantime, boil the skinned bananas (cut into chunks) in 2 pints (1.1 litres) of water for 20 minutes and strain the liquor into the bucket. Add 2 pints (1.1 litres) of water and leave to cool with a lid or cover on. When cool, add the other ingredients and the wine yeast and re-cover.

Ferment on the pulp for 5 or 6 days, stirring daily, then strain the liquor into a demijohn and fit a bung and airlock. Rack 10 days later and top up to the shoulder with water. Dissolve the rest of the sugar in wine, in stages as in the recipe on p. 52, to leave you with a sweet wine.

This wine is one that can be improved even further by adding 4 – 5 fl oz (115 – 140 ml) of brandy or vodka to the gallon (4.5 litres). If you do fortify the wine in this way, there should be so much alcohol in it that stabilising with potassium sorbate becomes unnecessary. This can, of course, be done with any sweet wine, but, as a general rule, is not practised by the majority of winemakers. There is little point in avoiding Excise duty by making your own wine and then buying expensive spirit to fortify it. In addition, such fortification with commercial spirit, or any blending with commercial wine, will disqualify your wine from the

great majority of classes in amateur wine competitions and shows. If you feel you need a little more alcohol, well then, just pour yourself another glass of your own pure homemade wine – you do know what it is made from.

Cherries

While we are on the subject, why not buy a few extra apricots, to put into your rumtopf for Christmas? Cherries too are particularly suited for inclusion in a rumtopf and will make a delicious wine as well. There are two main types of cherry

in the United Kingdom: the sweet or dessert cherry, a probable descendant of *Prunus avium*, and the sour or morello cherry, *P. cerasus*. *P. avium* is the wild cherry, or gean, which can be a full-sized tree, averaging 50 – 60 feet (15 – 18 m) in height. *P. cerasus* is a shrub-like growth, much-branched and freely producing suckers, and with fruit that is sour by comparison with the sweet cherries. Both are native to the United Kingdom, but selected varieties were introduced from the Near East by the Romans a thousand years ago and there has been a continual process of selection and breeding ever since. If you can only have one cherry tree, choose a morello, as sweet cherries are not self-fertile and a solitary sweet cherry tree will not produce fruit. Morello cherries are self fertile and are also suitable for pruning and training to fit within a suburban garden. There is an ancient fable that the Virgin Mary once wished to refresh herself with some sweet cherries from a tree. As it was a large tree the cherries were beyond her reach, so the branch itself bowed down to enable her to gather the fruit. Not many of us would qualify for such divine aid, and find it easier to grow and harvest the fruit of the sour cherry. That does sound more like sour grapes doesn't it?

SWEET MORELLO CHERRY WINE

4 lb (1.8 kg) cherries
3 ½ lb (1.6 kg) sugar
1 teaspoon (5 g) nutrient
1 teaspoon (5 g) tartaric acid
Pectic enzyme
Wine yeast

Pour 4 pints (2.3 litres) of boiling water over the de-stalked cherries and leave them to soak until cool. Crush the fruit by hand and remove the cherry stones that fall to the bottom of the bucket. Boil 3 lb (1.4 kg) or the sugar in 2 pints (1.1 litres) of water and add the solution to the bucket. When cool, add all the remaining ingredients, except the sugar. After 5 days, strain the liquor into a demijohn and continue the fermentation under airlock. In 2 weeks, rack if a heavy sediment of fruit pulp has formed.

When the fermentation has quietened down, dissolve the rest of the sugar in a little wine warmed in a pan, cool, and return it to the bulk. Leave it to ferment. If the wine ends up too dry for your palate, sweeten with a further 4 oz (115 g) of sugar dissolved in a little of the wine, and stabilise with a Campden tablet and a teaspoonful (5 g) of potassium sorbate.

If you take two-thirds of a bottle of this wine and one-third of a bottle of vodka, with a ½ teaspoonful (2,5 ml) of cherry brandy flavouring and a teaspoonful (5 ml) of glycerine, shake well and serve in small glasses, you will have a reasonable substitute for a commercial cherry brandy at a fraction of the cost. Why not put a bottle or two aside ready for those cold winter nights?

Peaches

Peaches begin to appear on the market from the beginning of July but they tend to be small, a little too firm and too expensive to consider as a winemaking ingredient. Towards the end of Summer, large juicy sweet peaches are cheap and plentiful and, as one good big peach will provide one bottle of wine, they are definitely among the best buys of the year. Peaches are eminently suitable for winemaking, having a good flavour and aroma, and yeast positively thrives in peach juice. 'Stuck' fermentations are virtually unheard of with this fruit and a good wine yeast will ferment remarkable quantities of sugar in a peach must.

There are a few dos-and-don'ts in the use of peaches for winemaking. Being so tender and juicy, they bruise very easily; they also pass the peak of ripeness very quickly. It is therefore most important that you ruthlessly cut away the slightest signs of damage and discard any over-ripe peaches. All fruit is simply a carrier for the seed, an attractor to help get the seed scattered and, after ripeness is achieved, natural enzymes start breaking down the fruit as the first stage of decay to release

the seed. In peaches, the first signs of enzymic action are the browning and softening of the flesh around the stone; this gives wine a bitter flavour, as does the oxidative browning that follows surface bruising. If you wish to make a good peach wine you need flawless fruit at its peak of perfection. Cheap fruit is often poor economy, if the quality of the fruit is less than first class. It is unlikely that many British winemakers grow sufficient peaches to have enough of the precous fruit to spare for making wine, so a visit to the wholesaler for a tray or two is the next best thing. If you can't buy wholesale, your local supermarket may sell you the fruit at a reduced price late on Saturday afternoon – the peaches may not keep till Monday. But at only six to eight peaches to the gallon (4.5 litres), depending on the size of the fruit, cost is not an important factor unless you are making 5 or 10 gallons (22.5 or 45 litres). If you have a choice, buy the best you can, the added expense is undoubtedly reflected in the quality of the finished wine.

You need not fear that you will have a useless surplus of peaches if you buy more than needed for winemaking. Quite apart from simply eating this luscious fruit, or making chutney or jam with them, you can also deep-freeze peaches quite successfully. A simple method is to peel the downy skin off the peaches, halve them so the stones can be removed, and then cut the fruit into slices or segments. Pour over them just enough sugar syrup to cover the slices; the syrup is simply 8 oz (225 g) of sugar in 1 pint (560 ml) of water, boiled and allowed to go cold. Pack the peaches and syrup in plastic freezer bags, with the air extracted, in quantities suitable for use at one meal. To serve, just allow to thaw and use as you would tinned peaches. The flavour is superb and you will have fresh fruit all the year around.

But first and foremost, peaches are for winemaking; here is a recipe that is certain to please.

SWEET PEACH WINE

6 – 8 peaches, depending on size
3 ½ lb (1.6 kg) sugar

91

2 teaspoons (10 g) pectic enzyme
1 teaspoon (5 g) Bentonite powder
1 teaspoon (5 g) tartaric acid
1 teaspoon (5 g) nutrient
1 (3 mg) Vitamin B tablet
Wine yeast – Tokay is recommended

Cut out any slight bruises or other damage to the fruit, then stone the peaches and lightly pulp them in a bucket. Pour over the pulp 4 pints (2.3 litres) of boiling water and stir to ensure the water reaches all the fruit pulp. Add 2¼ lb (1 kg) of sugar as syrup, boiled in 1 pint (560 ml) of water and leave to cool. Then stir in the acid, nutrient, pectic enzyme, Bentonite and Vitamin B tablet, and add the wine yeast.

Ferment on the pulp for 5 or 6 days, then strain without pressure into a demijohn and fit the bung and airlock. Rack after 2 weeks, to get rid of any fine fruit pulp sediment that came through the initial straining.

Leave to ferment down to a specific gravity of 1.000 – 1.005, then add a further 8 oz (225 g) of sugar, as syrup, and repeat this when the gravity drops again.

This wine may well ferment out to a dry wine, but it would be out of balance because of its high alcohol content. It is better to stabilise the wine after racking, with sulphite solution (1 teaspoonful/5 ml) and a ¼ teaspoonful (1.5 g) of potassium sorbate, and then sweeten it to taste. Top up to within an inch (25 mm) of the bung and leave to mature. When you can wait no longer, bottle the wine and it will be ready for drinking.

This wine can be improved a little by substituting 13 fl oz (365 g) of good white grape concentrate for the last 8 oz (225 g) of sugar. This is not necessary. The wine will be most enjoyable in any case, strong and luscious.

Finally, don't overlook adding to your rumtopf. Peaches, being soft, sweet and juicy are ideal for this purpose.

Plums

Another stone fruit available from homegrown trees is the plum, which has so many varieties that it is practically a group of fruits on its own. There are luscious plums like the Coe's Golden Drop or Victoria, rich and sweet, with honey-like juice almost bursting through its skin. There are cooking plums, such as the Pershore Egg from the Vale of Evesham, which crops so heavily that the branches often break off the tree if the wind blows. And there are numerous other plums and gages (named after Sir William Gage who grew greengages 200 years ago) and, of course, a variety of imported plums from the Continent.

All plums can be used for winemaking, but the sweet desert varieties are to be preferred. Cooking plums tend to have a higher acid content than dessert plums and as little as two thirds of the natural sugar content. What plums of all varieties do

have is a fair amount of pectin and a generous dose of pectin-destroying enzyme is advisable.

Because of the acidity of this fruit, 3 lb (1.4 kg) per gallon (4.5 litres) of wine is usually sufficient. More can be used and chemicals can be added to neutralise some of the acid. Precipitated chalk (calcium carbonate) will combine with the acids found in fruit juices and 1 level teaspoonful (4 g) will dispose of 1 part per thousand of acidity. Sodium bicarbonate can be used at the same rate; some foaming may occur in this process, so stand the demijohn in a bowl first. If you have a sensitive palate, you may find you can still taste these additives in the finished wine and, if so, it is obviously better not to exceed the recommended amount of fruit.

SWEET PLUM WINE

3 lb (1,4 kg) ripe dessert plums
3 ½ lb (1.6 kg) sugar
2 teaspoons (10 g) pectic enzyme
1 teaspoon (5 g) Bentonite powder
1 teaspoon (5 g) nutrient
1 (3 mg) Vitamin B tablet
Wine yeast

Rinse the fruit in a weak sulphite solution, strain, extract the stones and pulp the flesh of the plums. You may find it easier, depending on the plums, to simply pulp the whole fruit and collect the stones from the bottom of the bucket a day or so later. Don't leave them in the bucket too long or the flavour of the wine may be affected.

Pour over the plum pulp, 2 ¼ lbs (1 kg) of the sugar that has been boiled in 2 pints (1.1 litres) of water and allowed to go cold. Hot syrup or hot water should not be used on plums as the skins contain a waxy secretion that will dissolve with the heat. This forms a scummy surface on the must, preventing air from reaching the yeast in the early stages, or causes a haze in the wine that may prove most difficult to clear. Add 4 pints (2.3 litres) of water and stir in the yeast and all the other additives except the Bentonite and the surplus sugar. Cover and ferment on the pulp for 5 – 6 days stirring daily, then strain the liquid through a fine cloth into a demijohn. Do not squeeze the pulp, as this forces a lot of fine particles into the demijohn, which have to be cleared by racking when they eventually settle; in the meantime they may partially decay and give your wine an off flavour. Add the Bentonite and allow to ferment to dry, then add further doses of sugar as syrup, initially 8 oz (225 g), then subsequently in 4 oz (115 g) lots until you have used up the sugar. Stabilise and sweeten to taste if necessary.

A few plums left over? Stone them and use them in your rumtopf.

Dewberries

Dewberry, or dayberry is an antique name for the gooseberry. In Shakespeare's *A Midsummer Night's Dream* (III.i.165) Titania instructs the fairies Peas-Blossom, Cobweb, Moth and Mustard-seed to care for Bottom, to 'Feed him with apricocks and dewberries, with purple grapes, green figs and mulberries'. The dewberry, however, is also the name of some American brambles, which include *Rubus canadensis* and *R.alleghaniensis*, now hybridized and in cultivation, and last but not least, it is our own British native bramble, *R.caesius*, a slender trailing plant found on roadsides and banks, sandy heaths and wastes. Common in many parts of southern England, the dewberry becomes less frequent in the north, though it does grow extensively behind the coastal dunes of Wales, Merseyside and Lancashire.

The dewberry is a straggling plant, growing at ground level, with much weaker stems than those of its cousins, the blackberries, and slight prickles of little consequence – the dewberry is more likely to trip you than puncture your skin. The fruit is quite different from the blackberries, with only a few drupelets or segments, to each, purple to black in colour but usually covered with a white 'bloom'. The dewberry is much less fleshy than the blackberries, the pips are not so woody or so noticeable, but the juice, a brilliant red, flows freely and has a delicious flavour of its own. Dewberries are so juicy it is sometimes difficult to pick fully ripe berries without damaging them.

Because dewberries grow so close to the soil, picking more than a pound or so is a decided chore, but one that is well worthwhile. Pectin has to be added to make a

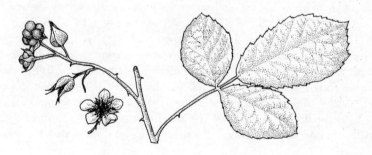

jam or jelly that sets well, but the fruit alone makes superb pies and wines with a remarkable degree of colour.

Dewberries ripen earlier than blackberries or most other wild fruits and make a good ingredient to harvest from the countryside during late Summer. If they grow nearby, use some to make a medium sweet wine. You will note that there is no added acid in this recipe; dewberries have enough acid of their own and, of course, some is also provided by the grape juice concentrate.

DEWBERRY SOCIAL WINE

2 lb (900 g) dewberries
2 ¼ lb (1 kg) sugar
1 pint (560 ml) red grape concentrate
1 teaspoon (5 g) pectic enzyme
1 teaspoon (5 g) Bentonite powder
1 teaspoon (5 g) nutrient
1 (3 mg) Vitamin B tablet
Burgundy wine yeast

Dissolve the sugar in 1 ½ pints (840 ml) of boiling water and allow to cool. Rinse the dewberries gently in a teaspoonful (5 ml) of sulphite solution (or a Campden tablet) in 1 pint (560 ml) of water. Drain the fruit, put it into a bucket and crush it. Pour in the grape concentrate, cool sugar syrup, 4 pints (2.3 litres) of cold water and all the other ingredients, including the yeast.

Ferment on the pulp for 4 or 5 days, stirring once or twice daily to break up the fruit cap, keeping the must covered for the rest of the time. Next, strain the must into a sterile demijohn, and fit a rubber bung and half-filled airlock.

Ten days later, rack the must off the sediment, to remove any fruit pulp fragments that might decay, top the jar up to the shoulder with water and leave the must to ferment to completion. Rack onto a teaspoonful (5 ml) of sulphite solution when the wine has cleared, stabilise it with a ¼ teaspoonful (1.5 g) of potassium sorbate and sweeten to taste with a little extra sugar.

One side effect of using sodium metabisulphite, either as a sulphite solution or Campden tablet is that the sulphur dioxide released is a bleach. This affects the colour of many red fruits, such as dewberries and blackberries, and may, if strong, bleach the colour away completely. Should this happen, don't worry. The fugitive colour will return when the sulphur dioxide level drops by dispersion into the air from the surface of the must.

This bleaching effect is a very convenient way of removing fruit juice stains from your hands after picking or sorting the berries. Before you wash your hands, rub them over with a little neat sulphite solution, keeping the fumes away from your face. This will take the colour away and soap and water will complete the job. Washing before using sulphite will fix the stain, which will blacken the skin and make the stain more difficult to remove.

The same process of dabbing with sulphite and then washing will remove fresh fruit stains from clothing quite effectively.

Beetroot

Beetroot is a well known ingredient for winemaking, but this probably stems from the days when imported fruit or juice was expensive, whereas beetroot was easily and cheaply grown and yielded a deep red-coloured juice when the root was cut. Beetroot wine is not as commonly made now as it used to be; unless you are very careful and use only 'baby beets', the wine has the same earthy flavour as the roots. This may fade away with long storage, by which time the colour will almost certainly have faded as well. Most old recipes for beetroot wine included cloves or ginger, or both, which gave the wine a slightly fiery taste and masked any off-flavours from the beet itself, or from the baker's yeast that had to be used.

Modern winemaking techniques and yeasts make such additives unnecessary and they should only be added if you particularly wish the wine to have that flavour.

Young beetroots – 'baby beet' – can be used to make this wine, before they acquire the coarse earthy flavour of the older roots.

MEDIUM SWEET BEETROOT WINE

3 – 4 lb (1.4 – 1.8 kg) young beetroot
6 cloves (or ½ oz [15 g] ginger) – optional
3 lb (1,4 kg) sugar
2 teaspoons (10 g) citric acid
1 teaspoon (5 g) nutrient
1 teaspoon (5 g) Bentonite powder
1 (3 mg) Vitamin B tablet
Wine yeast

Scrub the roots, and slice them into a pan with 2 pints (1.1 litres) of cold unsalted

water. Add up to six cloves or ½ oz (15 g) of ginger if desired, then slowly bring to the boil and simmer until tender; about 10 – 15 minutes should be enough.

Strain the hot liquor into your bucket and add 2¼ lb (1 kg) of sugar, stirring it well to dissolve the sugar. Add other ingredients and 4 pints (2.3 litres) of cold water. The must temperature should now be cool enough to add the yeast. Pour the must into a demijohn and fit a rubber bung and airlock.

Ferment until dry, then add the remainder of the sugar in two or three doses, stabilising and sweetening it at the end with a little extra sugar. Top up with water.

The wine is best stored for a few months to improve the flavour. Store it in the dark, or in a brown demijohn, to help preserve the rich purply-red colour, which will quickly go tawny in daylight.

Huckleberries

Though not common, winemakers do occasionally wish to make wine from huckleberries, and this gives rise to quite a lot of confusion. 'Huckleberry' is a common name for members of three different genera.

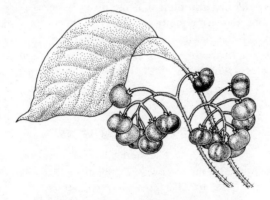

The *Gaylussacia* group are all from eastern North America and one member, *G. baccata*, is known as the black huckleberry. It is a small shrub with sweet, pleasantly flavoured berries, with ten seed-like nutlets in each berry. Other members of this family are also variously known as types of huckleberry and all are edible.

Of *Vaccinium*, the genus that includes the bilberries, cranberries and blueberries, *V. atrococcum* is also known as the black huckleberry and *V. vacillans* and *V. pennsylvanicum* are both known as the blue or sugar huckleberry, amongst numerous other names. All these are bushes.

Both the *Gaylussacia* and *Vaccinium* species are suitable for winemaking, and the bilberry wine recipe that follows.

The third type of huckleberry is commonly known as the garden huckleberry and is botanically identified as *Solanum intrusum*. Although this plant (note, not shrub) is a relative of the black nightshade and the bittersweet, it is nominally edible, even though it may contain poisonous alkaloids in small quantities. The garden huckleberry has a dull insipid flavour and, if you grow this plant from seed, the fruit is best used, if used at all, in combination with other ingredients that have a distinctive taste, such as blackberries and elderberries, in a mixed fruit wine.

Bilberries

As mentioned above, the genus *Vaccinium* includes *V.myrtillus*, a plant native to the United Kingdom and Europe generally and much better known as the bilberry. It grows wild, up to about 2 feet high (60 cm), on heaths and moorlands and acid ground around woodlands. The juicy blue-black fruit is up to ¼ inch (6 mm) in diameter, borne in the leaf axils singly or in pairs, and is laboriously slow to pick. Bilberries make a superb wine and, up to a few years ago, dried bilberries were one of the most popular winemaking ingredients. Unfortunately, the growing demand and inflation drove the price so high that the dried bilberries are no longer used. Bottled or fresh bilberries are equally good and, if the supply is limited, it is well worthwhile including bilberries in a mixed fruit wine to enhance the flavour.

Whortleberry is simply another name for bilberry, which is also sometimes called blaeberry, blueberry, whinberry and hurts, to mention just some of the alternatives.

BILBERRY SOCIAL WINE
3 lb (1.4 kg) fresh bilberries
2 lb (900 g) sugar initially plus sugar additions up to 1 lb (450 g)
1 pint (560 ml) red grape concentrate
1 teaspoon (5 g) tartaric acid
1 teaspoon (5 g) nutrient
1 teaspoon (5 g) pectic enzyme
1 (3 mg) Vitamin B tablet
Tokay or Burgundy wine yeast

Rinse the bilberries with a weak sulphite solution and drain. Crush the fruit sufficiently to break the skins, then pour over the berries 2 pints (1.1 litres) of boiling water and leave to cool. Boil the sugar to make a syrup with 1 pint (560 ml) of water and, when cool, pour this into the bucket with all the other ingredients and additives and 2 pints (1.1 litres) of cold water. Ferment on the pulp for 4 or 5 days, then strain into a demijohn and fit the bung and airlock. Rack after 14 days, then leave to ferment to dry.

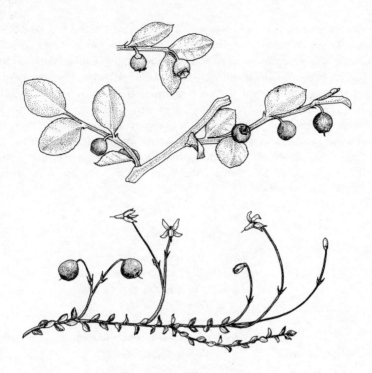

Boil up a further 1 lb (450 g) of sugar in ½ pint (280 ml) of water and add this, a ¼ pint (140 ml) at a time, each time the wine has fermented down to a specific gravity of about 1.005 or less. When the gravity has hardly altered 10 days after the last sugar addition, sweeten the wine to taste, add a teaspoonful (5 ml) of sulphite and a teaspoonful (5 g) of potassium sorbate and, if not clear, leave in a cool place for another week. Rack off the sediment, top up to 1 inch (25 mm) from the bung and replace the bung with a solid cork, soaked in hot water and sulphite to sterilise it. Leave to mature for 6 months if you can.

This makes a strong sweet wine, with plenty of alcohol and the fruity flavour that is found in port and similar dessert wines.

Bitter Beer

As a change from all these nice, sweet, and unfortunately fattening, wines, why not make a few gallons of bitter or stout? If you brew now you have the benefit of Summer's warmth to ensure a rapid fermentation, and a secondary fermentation in barrel or bottle to condition the beer, in a month or so you will have a good strong beer to ward off Autumn's chills and dampness.

As with the lagers, there are some really first-class canned hop concentrates and blends on the market and there is little to gain costwise in buying malt extract and hops or hop concentrates separately. The advantage is mainly in the freedom it gives you in brewing, for even starting with a set recipe you can easily vary it slightly, item by item, until the beer is just what you want. You then have a standard brew that you have developed to suit your own palate and it can be repeated fairly consistently as long as you adhere strictly to the recipe, use water from the same source, and stay with one supplier for your ingredients.

This time let us be a little more enterprising and make the beer from crushed pale malt, not malt extract, and some good British hops. The following recipe yields 5 gallons (22.5 litres) of beer.

BITTER BEER

5 lb (2.3 kg) crushed pale malt
4 oz (115 g) crushed crystal malt
4 oz (115 g) brewing flour
2 oz (60 g) Fuggles hops
1 oz (30 g) Goldings hops
1 teaspoon (5 g) Irish moss (copper finings)
10 oz (285 g) white sugar
6 oz (170 g) Demerara sugar
Beer yeast – top-fermenting

It is recommended that you buy your pale malt from a specialist shop that you know has a good turnover of stock. Crushed malt very quickly absorbs moisture from the air, which takes away its crisp, biscuit-crumb texture and leaves the malt 'slack'. Slack malt soon deteriorates, You can, of course, buy whole malt and crush it yourself, but you are unlikely to get the same consistent particle size that is required for good mashing.

Pour 5 pints (2.8 litres) of water into the pan you are using as a mash tun, and stir into it the pale malt, the crystal malt and the brewing flour, to make a thin porridgy slurry. Add a little more water if necessary. Bring to the boil and simmer for about 1½ hours at 150/152°F (65/67°C), stirring all the time. Test a few spots of the mash with brown iodine; if there is a blue stain reaction, the mashing must continue until the blue stain fails to appear on later tests. This stage of the mashing is known as 'reaching starch end point'.

Tip the mash into a large sieve lined with muslin and resting over a bucket top. When the wort has strained through the bed of malt, spray the malt with at least one, preferably two kettlefuls of boiling water and allow to drain. This is 'sparging'. The malt can now be discarded.

Pour the sweet wort back into the pan and add the hops and Irish moss. Bring to the boil and boil vigorously for half an hour at least. The Irish moss helps to coagulate the proteins in the wort, giving a bright clean beer when it has been fermented.

Put the sugars in your fermenting bin and, as you strain out the hops, run the sweet wort onto the sugar. Stir well to dissolve the sugar, then make up to 5 gallons (22.5 litres) with water. Pitch the yeast when the temperature is between 70 – 75°F (21 – 24°C) and cover.

The yeast will quickly multiply and, after a day or so, will be throwing out surpluses as a stiff foam that piles up on top of the beer. Skim this off and with a sterile damp cloth wipe away the ring of coarse hop resins that forms on the side of the bin.

Continue the fermentation for about 4 or 5 days, by which time it will have quietened down considerably. Run it off into one large container which can be fitted with an airlock, or into demijohns, for a couple more days to finish fermenting. At this stage, there will be only a sprinkling of bubbles on the surface of the beer, few bubbles rising and the beer will have started clearing from the surface downwards. Stir in a dose of beer finings in accordance with the instructions on the packet or bottle and leave for 24 hours at least.

Rack the young beer off the sediment, stirring in ¼ pint (140 ml) of standard sugar syrup (1 lb/450 g to ½ pint/280 ml water). If you prefer, add a ½ teaspoonful (2.5 g) of dry sugar to each 1 pint (560 ml) bottle, through a dry funnel, before bottling the beer. Cap and, if dry sugar has been used, give each bottle a shake to dissolve the priming sugar.

Keep the bottled beer in a warm place for 2 or 3 days to develop condition, then transfer it to a cool place to deposit the tiny bit of fresh yeast in the bottom of the bottle. Leave the beer at least 2 or 3 weeks to mature.

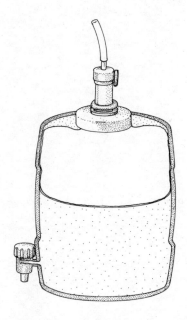

The beer can instead be run into a keg or small plastic barrel to condition and clear in the same way with the priming sugar. The yeast deposited should all be below the level of the tap. Barrelled beer will naturally take longer to clear than a smaller quantity of beer, and there are pipes that can be fitted to the back of the tap, rising to a float near surface level. This allows you to draw clear beer while the lower part of the barrel, at tap level, may still be cloudy. An undoubted boon to the thirsty brewer who had no stocks to draw on!

As you drink the beer in the barrel, an ever-increasing part of the barrel becomes empty. If nothing can get into the barrel to replace the beer drawn off, a partial vacuum is formed and the beer will cease to flow.

If air can get in to replace the beer, it will not be long before the unsterile air brings with it wild yeasts or bacteria, with the obvious results of gallons of spoiled beer. The most popular solution to this problem is to fit a carbon dioxide bottle, varying in size from Sparklet bulbs upwards; the inert gas will then form a sterile blanket over the beer. It is not there to pressurise the beer and force it out of the barrel.

An alternative is to use one of the systems available that depend on a large rubberized balloon that has a valved inlet pipe. The balloon or bag is put inside the barrel, with the inlet pipe leading through the cap of the barrel. As the beer is drunk so the balloon is blown up by mouth, remaining constantly in contact with the surface of the beer. As the replacement air is inside the balloon, the beer cannot be infected by the bacteria it carries. This is a nice simple system, which does not rely on bottles of high-pressure gas.

However you process the finished beer, you will wonder why you never made such a delectable brew before.

AUTUMN

Apples

From September onwards, there comes, freshly available, the new crop of one of the most versatile of all winemaking ingredients, the apple. Apples can be used to make cyder, light Germanic white table wines, pleasing social wines, heavy dessert wines and sherry-type wines. Apple juice can be added to virtually any other recipe to give a little more body and flavour; in fact the apple is the perfect all-the-year-round general ingredient.

Apples belong to the genus *Malus*, which includes a wide range of fruits that are all perfectly acceptable for winemaking. You may, of course, use dessert apples and cooking apples. These may be the perfect fruit you harvest, but equally may be damaged or blemished fruit (as long as the damaged parts are cut out and discarded), or the windfalls of unripe fruit brought down by early gales. These familiar apples are all quite suitable for our purposes, but so also are varieties of apples that each year rot in their tons simply because their value or suitability is not realised. There are many varieties of apple grown simply for their spring blossom, or the colourful display of foliage or fruit. These are the many varieties and species of crab-apple, from the well-known crabs, such as John Downie and Golden Hornet, to the small, hard, purple-red fruits popularly known as 'Siberian' crabs. In these, the little cherry-like fruit is stained throughout with the same purple pigment as the skin. They are true apples, though, with little apple-seeds in the core, and can be used in just the same way as any other apple. Additionally, there are larger ornamental apples, like the Wisley Crab, that probably have a dry mealy flesh, and these two can be used as an ingredient, preferably blended with other, sharper-flavoured, apples.

Lastly, but not to be overlooked, are the native wild crab-apples found in hedges

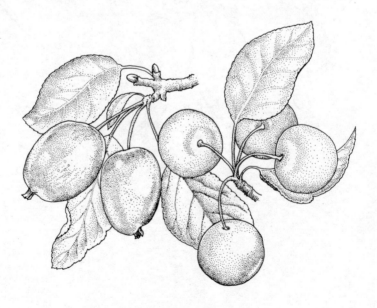

and the edges of woodlands. These apples are usually very acid, but mellow if kept until well into the winter. Wild crabs blend well with blander apples grown at home in the garden.

Imported apples are available all the year round, as too are dried and canned apples and bottled and carton-packed juices, and these can be used at any time as a substitute for the freshly harvested homegrown apples, though the latter are to be preferred, both for quality and cost.

Taking the first apples available, the windfalls, we can make a pleasing hock-style wine, using to our advantage the sharp crisp flavour of the partly ripened fruit. The dominant acid in apples is malic acid, which has a slightly sour and fruity flavour.

LIGHT TABLE APPLE WINE

3 lb (1.4 kg) windfalls, crabs and mixed apples
½ pint (280 ml) white grape concentrate
1 ¾ lb (790 g) white sugar
1 teaspoon (5 g) nutrient
½ teaspoon (2.5 g) tartaric acid
1 ½ teaspoons (7.5 g) pectic enzyme
1 (3 mg) Vitamin B tablet
White wine yeast

Rinse the apples in dilute sulphite solution and cut out any damaged or bruised parts. Crush coarsely, just sufficiently to allow liquids to soak into the fruit, by pounding the apples in the bucket, a few at a time, with the end of a rolling-pin, a bottle filled with water to weight it or a smooth block of hardwood. Little crab-apples need only be halved or quartered, if this is easier. Cover at once with the sugar as a cold solution, plus 5 pints (2.8 litres) of cold water. Add all the other ingredients, including the yeast, stir well and cover. Stir twice daily for 5 days, then strain off the liquid must through a fine cloth bag into a demijohn. Fit a rubber bung and airlock and leave in a warm place for 2 weeks. The wine will by then probably have thrown down a thick deposit, mainly a slurry of fruit pulp. The must should be racked off this sediment, which will otherwise eventually decay and give the wine an off-flavour.

Return the wine to the clean demijohn, top up with cold water and refit the bung and airlock; leave the wine to finish fermenting, preferably well away from bright light. When the wine falls clear and the sugar has all been consumed (SG 1.000 or less), rack it again onto a crushed Campden tablet, or 1 teaspoonful (5 ml) of sulphite solution, and a teaspoonful (5 g) of potassium sorbate. The wine can then be slightly sweetened to taste and bottled. This type of wine can be drunk young and will not benefit from more than a few month's maturation.

A variation on this recipe is to add a large pinch of dried elderflower, or one frozen head, in a piece of muslin or fine nylon cloth, and let it soak in the wine for 2 or 3 days before the wine is bottled. This will improve the bouquet which would take some time to develop naturally during storage, and which will be reminiscent of the bouquet of some Mosel wines.

This recipe relies on crushing the apples and quickly submerging them with the sugar syrup and water. This technique reduces the chance of the apples browning due to oxidation by exposure to the air. Apples that have been allowed to brown this way will produce a darker-coloured juice and, eventually, a darker wine, and the flavour is also liable to be affected. Neither of these effects is wanted in a light white wine, but both may deliberately be sought when making a strong dessert wine or a sherry-type wine from apples.

If you have a deep-freeze chest, then the apples can be frozen for a few days in the storage compartment. Don't put them in the quick-freezing section; slow freezing produces coarser ice crystals that disrupt the fruit cells and so, after thawing, the apples are soft and pulpy; the juice can then be squeezed out of them easily. The juice should be used at once or returned to the freezer for storage as blocks of frozen juice until required.

APPLE DESSERT WINE

6 lb (2.8 kg) mixed apples
1 lb (450 g) raisins
2¼ lb (1 kg) sugar initially plus approx. 1 lb (450 g) added later
2 teaspoons (10 g) pectic enzyme
1 teaspoon (5 g) nutrient
1 (3 mg) Vitamin B tablet
¼ teaspoon (1.5 g) magnesium sulphate (Epsom salts)
Wine yeast – active, such as Tokay

Rinse the fruit in dilute sulphite solution and discard any damaged parts. Crush or juice the apples into a sterile bucket and at once add 4 pints (2.3 litres) of cold water. Boil 2¼ lb (1 kg) of sugar in 1½ pints (840 ml) of water, allow it to cool and add it to the bucket. Put in the raisins, chopped or minced, and all the other ingredients and cover the bucket with a lid or a polythene sheet or bag. Open and stir daily, to break up the cap of fruit that will form due to the crushed apple and raisins being lifted by the fermentation gases.

After a week, strain the must into a demijohn and fit the bung and airlock. Rack 2 weeks later, but do not top up with cold water. Instead add ½ pint (280 ml) of sugar syrup (the syrup being made by boiling the other 1 lb (450 g) of sugar in ½ pint (280 ml) of water and letting it cool). Keep the rest of the syrup in a stoppered bottle, adding ¼ pint (140 ml) each time the wine ferments to dry. It may be necessary to make up a little more syrup of the same strength to sweeten the wine when fermentation ends. At this stage, the wine should be racked, a crushed Campden tablet or a teaspoonful (5 ml) of sulphite solution added, and a teaspoonful (5 g) of potassium sorbate stirred well in, before the wine is sweetened to taste.

This will be a strong, full-bodied wine to be drunk in moderation, and should have a sweet finish to balance it. It is well worth maturing in bulk for a few months before bottling.

A sherry-style wine can be made the same way, using say 4 lb (1.8 kg) of apples, adding a true Sherry Flor yeast and a teaspoonful (5 g) of gypsum. As the fermentation quietens down after the first few weeks, replace the bung and airlock with a hard plug of compressed unmedicated cotton wool. As long as this material is kept dry, it will filter out wild yeasts etc. while allowing oxygen into the air-space above the shoulder of the jar. If you are very fortunate, a surface layer of sherry 'flor' may develop, to give a true sherry flavour. In such a case, the wine should be left undisturbed until this complex blend of surface-living yeasts breaks up and sinks. In most cases, the sherry yeast will ferment in the normal way; some oxidation of the wine will produce some of the acetaldehydes that contribute towards the sherry flavour. This is the major instance of the tendency of apples to oxidise quickly being a benefit to the winemaker, instead of a hindrance.

This sherry-type wine should be sulphited, stabilised with potassium sorbate, and sweetened to taste in the usual manner. Long maturation after bottling is not necessary.

If the wine is solely for home consumption, and not for entering in any competitive show, it is often helpful to add a bottle of commercial sherry to your homebrew; this will enhance the flavour of the whole gallon to a surprising degree.

Blackberries

The ubiquitous blackberry ripens in the Autumn and this well-known fruit is an excellent winemaking ingredient. There are several *Rubus* species, collectively known as blackberries, in the United Kingdom, with *R. fruticosus* probably being the most common. Our Victorian forebears recognised several score of species, but these are now accepted as hybrids and local variants in the majority of cases. One easily identified species is R. *laciniatus*, the cultivated cut-leaved or parsley-leaved blackberry, and there are also prickle-free cultivars available for garden planting, such as the Merton thornless. All species and varieties of blackberry can equally well be used for winemaking, or any other culinary use, though it is important to gather only fruit that is fully ripened. English folklore has it that, after Michaelmas Day (September 29th), Old Nick has either put his cloven hoof on blackberries or has spat on them. Whatever the cause, late-picked blackberries will often prove to be full of little white maggots that may not show until the fruit is being washed and picked over at home.

Members of the blackberry group are generally well balanced for acid, tannin, flavour and colour, and not too high in pectin. They do, however, tend to carry persistent wild yeasts and mildew spores and it is important that the fruit is thoroughly rinsed in a fairly strong sulphite bath (1 pint/560 ml of water containing either two Campden tablets or 2 teaspoonfuls/10 ml of sulphite solution). Alternatively, the fruit can simply be rinsed to remove odd leaves, insects, etc., and then simmered for 10 minutes in near boiling water.

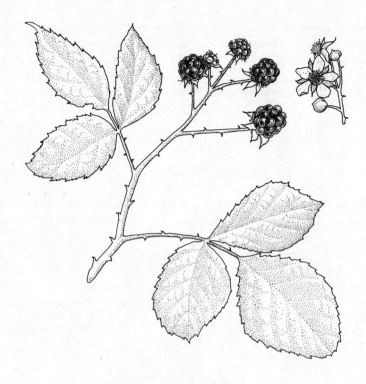

DRY RED BLACKBERRY TABLE WINE

3 lb (1.4 kg) ripe blackberries
½ pint (280 ml) red grape concentrate
2¼ lb (1 kg) white granulated sugar
1 teaspoon (5 g) nutrient
1 teaspoon (5 g) pectic enzyme
Bordeaux wine yeast

Pick over the fruit in a sulphite bath, removing stray stalks, damaged berries and other unwanted fragments, and roughly crush the fruit in a sterile bucket. Do not crush the seeds, as the seed contents will coarsen the flavour of the wine.

Boil up the sugar in 1½ pints (say 1 litre) of water, and pour while hot over the crushed berries. Stir and leave for a few minutes, then add 4 pints (2.8 litres) of cold water and the remaining ingredients, except the yeast and pectic enzyme. Check that the temperature is down to 80°F (27°C) before these are added, then stir them in and fit the bucket lid.

Stir daily for 5 or 6 days, then strain off the pulp, pressing lightly, into a demijohn. Rack 10 days later and top up with cold water.

Leave to ferment to dry, then rack onto sulphite, and potassium sorbate if the wine needs sweetening slightly. Alternatively, the sweetening can be done with glycerine or a non-fermenting sugar substitute, in which case the sorbate can be omitted. Bottle and store to mature, preferably for some months to get the best from the wine, though of course it can be drunk while fairly young.

Blackberry wines tend to become tawny with age and maturation, even if stored away from the light. The blackberry is therefore particularly suited to making heavy sweet dessert wines, full-bodied and high in alcohol, where a slight tawniness is not amiss and its fruity flavour shows to advantage.

BLACKBERRY DESSERT WINE

5 – 6 lb (2.3 – 2.8 kg) blackberries
1 pint (560 ml) red grape concentrate
8 oz (225 g) Demerara Sugar
2 lb (900 g) white granulated sugar
1 teaspoon (5 g) nutrient
1 teaspoon (5 g) pectic enzyme
1 (3 mg) Vitamin B tablet
1 heaped teaspoon (6 g) Bentonite powder
Wine yeast – good

Wash, clean and sterilise the fruit, continuing as in the previous recipe, filling only to the shoulder of the jar.

A month after the first racking, check the specific gravity of the wine, and if below SG 1.005 dissolve 4 oz (115 g) of sugar in a little of the wine, warmed in a pan, and add it to the demijohn. Stir well and record the new specific gravity. Check again a month later and, if the specific gravity has again dropped to 1.005, add a further 4 oz (115 g) of sugar. This can be repeated perhaps once more – if you have a very active yeast; the fermentation will slow down sooner or later and the wine should then be racked, sulphited and treated with potassium sorbate to prevent any further yeast activity. The wine should be sweet, luscious and well worth maturing. Do keep at least three or four bottles of this wine for a few months; if you make a written note of your tastings of the young wine, you will be surprised at how much it will have developed when you open a bottle and taste it critically in 6 months' time.

Elderberries

Another group, the elders (*Sambucus* spp.), are widely scattered round the world, mainly in the northern hemisphere, with some – particularly in North America – being developed under cultivation until they merit being grown as a commercial fruit crop. In the United Kingdom, there are only two native species and one, the dwarf elder (*S. ebulus*) is to be avoided as it is quite inedible. It is also known as Danewort, from an old belief that it sprung up wherever the Danes, who raided this country in the ninth century, shed blood. As it is only low-growing, it is unlikely to be confused with the common elder (*S. nigra*), which is a good thing in view of its harsh purgative properties.

By contrast, the common elder is probably one of the best known shrubs or small trees in the country. Harvest the clusters of glossy black berries when the heads start to hang downwards – a sign that the fruit is ripe. Occasionally, you may find bushes whose berries display the evidence of ripeness, but may be any colour from a pale greeny-white to a golden-red. These are just aberrant forms in which the pigment that makes the normal berries black has developed only partially, or not at all. The berries are still quite usable and some interesting variations on elderberry wine can be made from them. Such wines occasionally prove difficult to clear. It may also prove necessary with these pale berries to add a little grape tannin or cold tea if the must tastes too bland; this varies according to the tree of origin.

SWEET SOCIAL ELDERBERRY WINE

3 lb (1.4 kg) fresh or frozen elderberries
½ pint (280 ml) red grape concentrate (or 8 oz/225 g chopped raisins)
3 lb (1.4 kg) white sugar
1 teaspoon (5 g) nutrient
1 teaspoon (5 g) pectic enzyme
1 ½ teaspoons (7.5 g) tartaric acid
1 teaspoon (5 g) Bentonite powder
Wine yeast

The fruit can conveniently be stripped from the head by combing it with the tines of a tablefork. Rinse the berries in sulphite, drain, and crush them in the bucket. Boil the sugar with 1 ½ pints (840 ml) of water and pour it hot over the berries. Add 4 pints (2.3 litres) of cold water and, when the temperature is down to 80°F (27°C) add all the other ingredients and the yeast. Cover and stir daily for 5 or 6 days, then strain into a demijohn and top up to just above the shoulder of the jar with water. Fit the bung and

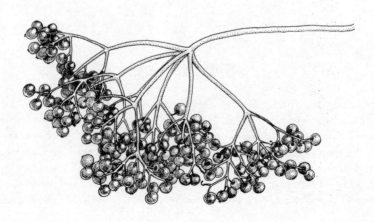

airlock and leave undisturbed for 10 – 14 days. Rack the wine then, and leave to ferment out. The wine should then be racked again, and stabilised and sweetened in the usual way.

An alternative is to allow the wine to ferment down to the required sweetness and then rack the wine onto a crushed Campden tablet or a teaspoonful (5 ml) of sulphite solution. Repeat this a week later and stabilise with a heaped teaspoonful (5 g) of potassium sorbate. Leave the wine with a plug of cottonwool in the neck of the demijohn for a few days to allow some of the sulphite fumes to disperse in the air. This wine can be drunk fairly soon, but improves with keeping.

Elderberries can be used to make good table wines, but it is recommended that the fruit – say 3 lb to the gallon (1.4 kg to 4.5 litres) – is simmered in water for 15 minutes and then made up in the same way as the dry red blackberry table wine p. 108. Dessert wines too can be made with elderberries, but the large quantity of elderberries used means that the wine will be very high in harsh tannins and may take years to mature to a smooth wine that doesn't pucker your mouth. This fruit undoubtedly can play its part in dessert wines, but ideally as one fruit in a blend of fruits. An excellent port-style recipe including elderberries appears on p. 112.

As well as fresh and frozen elderberries harvested by him or herself, the amateur winemaker can purchase dried elderberries at any time of the year. As the extraction of moisture reduces the weight of dried fruit, only one-quarter of the amount recommended in fresh fruit recipes is required. Dried elderberries do not make as good a wine as fresh fruit, but should not be disregarded as they are one of the few materials for making red wine that are always available. See the recipe for dried elderberry and rosehip wine on p. 65.

Damsons

Members of the great group of stoned fruits belonging to the genus *Prunus* ripen at this time of year. The cultivated damson *(P. damascena)*, with its dark blue fruit lightened by a bloom of wild yeasts is ready for use and, in favourable years, produces huge crops that make superb wines, jams and jellies. Its wild counterpart, the bullace, is a

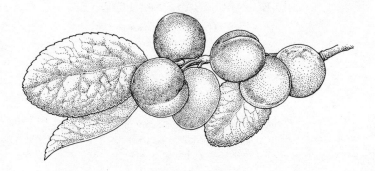

subspecies of damson *(P. damascena institia)* yet has a quite different flavour and can vary from yellow through to damson-coloured when ripe. The bullace, in the author's experience, tends to have an odd, almost musky, aroma and taste when fermented and it is suggested that, if you wish to make bullace wine, you should restrict your first attempt to just 1 gallon (4.5 litres) until you can taste the finished wine. Surplus fruit can be deep-frozen in the usual way if you wish to store it until its fate is decided, i.e. either to make more bullace wine or just to throw the fruit away.

DAMSON SOCIAL WINE

3 lb (1.4 kg) ripe damsons
3 lb (1.4 kg) sugar
½ pint (280 ml) red grape concentrate
1 teaspoon (5 g) nutrient
1½ teaspoons (7.5 g) pectic enzyme
¼ teaspoon (1.5 g) magnesium sulphate (Epsom salts)
1 (3 mg) Vitamin B tablet
Bordeaux wine yeast

If you want the wine to have a good red colour you should also include 2 oz (60 g) of dried or 8 oz (225 g) fresh or frozen elderberries or bilberries.

Soak all the fruit in a weak sulphite solution for a day, then drain it and crush the fruit gently. Extract all loose damson stones and discard them. Make a syrup of the sugar and 2 pints (1.1 litres) of boiling water and allow it to cool. Add this syrup and all the other ingredients and the yeast to the bucket, as well as a further 4 pints (2.3 litres) of water. Ferment on the pulp for 5 or 6 days, stirring daily, and strain through a coarse cloth into a demijohn. Fit a rubber bung and airlock and leave for 2 weeks before racking. Next, top up the jar with water and leave until the fermentation ends. Rack onto a teaspoonful (5 ml) sulphite solution and a ¼ teaspoonful (1.5 g) of potassium sorbate, sweeten to taste as a medium sweet wine (SG about 1.010 – 1.015) and bottle.

The following recipe combines the best characteristics of blackberry, elderberry and damson, and makes a rich sweet port-style wine that does not require months or years of maturation before becoming drinkable. It is a luxury brew, but well worth making.

MIXED PORT-STYLE FRUIT WINE

2¼ lb (1 kg) elderberries
1½ lb (675 g) damsons
1 lb (450 g) dewberries or blackberries
2¼ lb (1 kg) can of red grape concentrate
2¼ lb (1 kg) sugar
1 teaspoon (5 g) nutrient
1 teaspoon (5 g) pectic enzymes
1 (3 mg) Vitamin B tablet
Wine yeast – strong

For the yeast, avoid port yeasts, for these are not naturally high-alcohol tolerant yeasts. Port only ferments for a few days, after which the yeast is knocked out by a massive addition of grape spirit. It is better to use say, a Tokay yeast, or even a good strain of Bordeaux or Burgundy yeast.

Rinse the fruit in a sulphite and water bath, strain off the liquid and crush the fruit. To the fruit pulp, add all the other ingredients, except 12 oz (340 g) of the sugar. Make the sugar up as a syrup and cool it before adding it to the bucket. Add 4 pints (2.3 litres) of water and leave to ferment, stirring daily for 6 days.

Strain the liquid into a demijohn, fitting a bung and airlock, and rack a fortnight later. At that stage, add a further 8 oz (225 g) of sugar as syrup before topping up with water.

When the fermentation ends, the remaining 4 oz (115 g) of sugar can be used for sweetening if required, after the wine has been racked, sulphited, and stabilised with a teaspoonful (5 g) of potassium sorbate. Bottle and resist as long as possible!

Sloes

The last common member of the plum group is the sloe, fruit of the blackthorn (*P. spinosa*) and usually quite astringent in taste, but suitable for blending with other

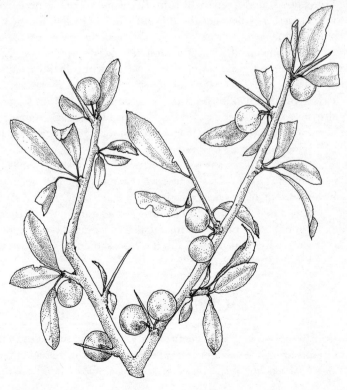

fruits for winemaking. Blackthorn bushes have for centuries provided walking sticks, tea substitutes and leather dyes, but nowadays the most popular produce is probably sloe gin.

Sloes or damsons can be used to flavour gin and turn it into what is virtually a sweet liqueur. Prick the fruit all over with a fork and put it into a Kilner jar or other screw-top bottle. Add 6 oz (170 g) of sugar for each pound (450 g) of fruit, then add sufficient gin to cover it. Screw the lid down and shake the jar to start dissolving the sugar. Shake daily until the sugar has all been absorbed, then put the jar away for 6 weeks or so to allow the gin to extract the colour and flavour from the fruit.

Pour off the liquid and filter it through a linen cloth or coarse filter paper. It can then be put in a bottle and stored away until Christmas. Similar drinks can be made with other fruits when they are in season, e.g. cherries soaked in brandy, or sweet plums put down in vodka. Apart from sloes, which are rather harshly-flavoured, any such fruit can be added to a rumtopf or used as a base for a fruit crumble.

Marrow

Each year, the winemaking press includes at least one reader's enquiry about the ancient and romantic-sounding marrow rum. In theory, all that is necessary is to cut off one end of a marrow, scoop out the soft pulp and seeds and fill the cavity with brown sugar and a little baker's yeast. One then replaces the end as a cap and supports or hangs the marrow on end. Insert a straw into the lower end of the marrow, leading to a bowl placed beneath it; this should then slowly fill with a highly alcoholic liquor.

If you have read the foregoing pages attentively you will quickly realise that this is a folklore tale, a myth that cannot be true. In practice you will find that the straw constantly drips a solution of juice and dissolved brown sugar, containing a small amount of alcohol in its later stages. The marrow simply goes soggier each day and, often as not, develops a fine case of mildew.

If you have a surplus of marrows and feel you positively must try to make a marrow wine, then dice 4 or 5 lb (1.8 – 2.3 kg) of scooped out marrow, and ferment on the pulp in the usual way with sugar, nutrient, pectic enzyme and a wine yeast. Add the juice of two large oranges and a lemon and 1 oz (30 g) of root ginger, which should be well crushed with a pair of pliers or beaten with a mallet. The sugar can include some soft brown or Demerara to help the flavour and the wine should be stabilised and finally sweetened (SG 1.020 approximately).

Christmas Ale

Now is the time to make a heavy strong beer for Christmas, one that should only be drunk in half-pints or nips. Such a beer can be made from the following recipe. As it contains 12% – 13% alcohol, it is a beer that needs a couple of months in the bottle to mature and will, in fact, keep for several years. It is very strong for a beer; don't let your guests risk losing their driving licences through drinking more than a glass of it.

CHRISTMAS ALE

3 lb (1.4 kg) medium dried malt extract (or 1 lb/450 g light and 2 lb/900 g dark)
1 lb (450 g) crushed crystal malt
4 oz (115 g) English hops
3 lb (1.4 kg) white sugar
2 lb (900 g) soft brown or Demerara sugar
Beer yeast – good top-fermenting type

This recipe is for 4½ gallons (20.5 litres) but can of course be scaled down proportionately to make a smaller brew.

The crystal malt can be cracked by covering it with a teatowel and part-crushing it with a rolling-pin, by passing it through a coarse-bladed mincer, or even by putting a few ounces at a time for a few seconds in a liquidiser. Do not overdo this and reduce the malt to a powder, or you may have problems in straining it out later.

If you have a large enough container, boil all the malts and the hops in 1½ gallons (about 7 litres) of water for half an hour. If you don't have a large enough pan, then divide the ingredients into two or even three boilings, but be sure to put some of the hops in each batch.

Place the sugars in the fermenting bin, reserving 4 oz (115 g) for conditioning, and, after arranging a straining cloth over the bin, tip in the contents of your pan or pans. A lot of the sweet wort will be trapped in the malt husks and the spent hops, and should be washed out by rinsing them with a couple of kettles of hot water. This is the process known as sparging. The solids can then be discarded.

Stir the contents of the bin well to dissolve the sugar, then add cold water to bring the level up to 4½ gallons (20.5 litres). Check that the wort temperature has dropped to 75°F (24°C) or less before adding the yeast, either stirred in if a starter bottle has been prepared or sprinkled over the surface if a dried yeast is used. Cover carefully to exclude any contaminants, as beer is very susceptible to infections, particularly in the early stages.

Within a day or so, the yeast will form a thick creamy head, which should be skimmed off. A dark brown ring will probably be deposited on the bin at the liquid level; this is largely unwanted coarse-flavoured hop resins and should be wiped away with a clean cloth dampened with sulphite solution to preserve the beer's flavour.

After a week, syphon the beer into containers that can be fitted with airlocks. Rack again a week later and then thoroughly stir in the 4 oz (115 g) of sugar dissolved in a little boiling water. Top up with water to make good any losses through racking, stir again and bottle. Only unchipped returnable bottles that have been made for carbonated drinks, such as beer, cider or fizzy 'pop', should be used. 'One-trip' non-returnable bottles should be thrown away for safety's sake. Over the years, the dissolved dextrins in the beer will slowly ferment, contributing to the condition arising from the added sugar, so it is most unwise to take any unnecessary risks when bottling.

When drinking beer that is more than 2 or 3 months old, it helps to chill it for half an hour or so before opening the bottles to prevent excess foaming.

Medlar

Late Autumn brings varied fruits, some common, some unusual. The medlar *(Mespilus germanica)* is found mainly in the southern counties of the United Kingdom, and is a strange and ancient tree that bears thorns in the wild, although there are none on cultivated varieties. The 'Dutch' and 'Monstrous' varieties have the largest fruits, though it is said that the larger the tree, the larger the fruit. The medlar is not native to the United Kingdom and is believed to have been introduced by the Romans. The fruit is odd in that the lower end, where the flower sepals remain, never completely closes up and the seeds can be seen inside the cavity. Medlars change from green to a golden brown when they ripen in warmer countries, but in the United Kingdom they usually need to undergo a process known as 'bletting'. This simply means that the fruit is picked as late as possible and stored in single layers in trays or on shelves until it darkens and softens. The pulp of what is really a partially decayed fruit is then ready to eat, with cream, and is more palatable than it might sound. Medlars, bletted or not, can be used for winemaking and have proved to be better when still fairly firm, like a fully ripe apple. Make it up as for apple wine; it will be fairly sweet when finished. Medlars will hybridise with hawthorn and the usual method of propagation is to graft them onto hawthorn, pear or quince.

Quince

Quince, too, is a tree that is less commonly found than in past years. The true fruiting quince *(Cydonia oblonga)* grows to 15 – 20 ft (4.5 – 6 m) and bears knobbly fruit, rather like green apples. It has been cultivated since at least the seventh century BC, being mentioned in the marriage rites laid down by the Greek sage, Solon. This fruit has a very strong, aromatic and spicy flavour and, although wine can be made from the fruit

alone, most winemakers prefer to blend quinces with apples, commonly in the proportion of one part quince to three parts apple.

A similar fruit grows on the ornamental flowering quince *(Chaenomeles japonica)*, whose bright red flowers often brighten the winter months in sheltered sites. This quince is perfectly acceptable and can be used in precisely the same way as the larger variety, with the advantage of a much wider distribution in gardens.

Pear

Pears are used in a very similar way to apples, but are very prone to produce off-flavours and cloudy wines if precautions are not taken. Firstly, pears should be used while still firm; pears that are fully ripe – 'sleepy' is a popular description – will break down in the fermenting bucket and the wine will be difficult to clear. For the same reason, pears for winemaking should not be cooked or sterilised with boiling

117

water; rely on sulphite and cold water for the juice extraction. The skins of pears are high in tannin and half the fruit should be peeled and the skins discarded. Finally, the proportions and ingredients for apple wine are suitable for pears, except that a further teaspoonful (5 g) of tartaric acid should be added. Pectic enzyme and a teaspoonful (5 g) of Bentonite are always required to ensure clarity.

Rosehips

One of Autumn's most common and always attractive fruits is the wild rosehip, borne in clusters on the briars of the native roses, mainly the dog-rose *(Rosa canina)*. Garden roses will, of course, produce hips also, but rose-growers usually dead-head the fading blooms to encourage a further flush of flowers to grow. There are a few species of roses that produce large numbers of hips which ripen satisfactorily, e.g. *Rosa Moyesii*, with

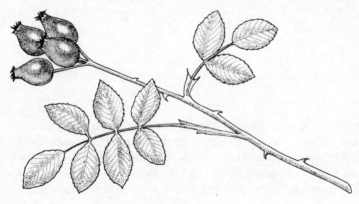

its pendant hips, bright orange-red, like elegant vases suspended from its slender flower stalks, or the flatter *R. rugosa* hips, reminiscent of small tomatoes. All rosehips are good fermenting material when ripe, and even the thorniest briars can be harvested of sufficient hips for a gallon of wine in half an hour or less. You will probably suffer a few pricks and scratches, but it is all in a good cause.

Rosehips can be used on their own, or in a variety of blends, but probably the most widely known and deservedly popular combination is rosehip and fig. These two ingredients blend beautifully together to make rich, sweet wines reminiscent of Marsala and brown sherry. Gather your hips as late as possible, to ensure ripeness; an early frost helps break down the hard shiny rind of the hip. If you fear the birds are enjoying the harvest before you, the rosehips can be gathered and frosted artificially for a day or so in a deep freeze or the frozen-food compartment of a refrigerator.

SWEET SOCIAL ROSEHIP AND FIG WINE

2 lb (900 g) rosehips
6 oz (170 g) dried figs
2 ¼ lb (1 kg) granulated sugar initially
1 teaspoon (5 g) citric acid
1 teaspoon (5 g) pectic enzyme
1 teaspoon (5 g) nutrient
¼ teaspoon (1.5 g) grape tannin (or a cup of strong tea)
Sherry yeast or General Purpose wine yeast

De-stalk the rosehips and rinse with a weak sulphite and water mixture. Drain the hips and crush or coarsely mince them. Chop or break up the figs and place the rosehips, figs, sugar, acid, nutrient and tannin in the fermenting bucket.

Pour over them 6 pints (3.4 litres) of boiling water, stir well and cover. When the contents of the bucket have cooled to 80°F (27°C) or below, add the pectic enzyme and the yeast. Re-cover and stir daily for a week, then strain into a demijohn and fit the bung and airlock. Rack 10 days later and top up just to the shoulder with water if necessary.

Check the progress of the fermentation, either by taste or (better) by hydrometer, and each time the wine tastes almost dry, or the specific gravity drops to 1.005 or less,

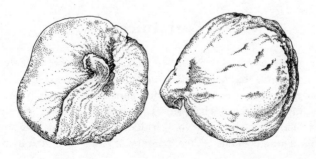

add a further 4 oz (115 g) of sugar dissolved in a little of the wine warmed in a pan. When the gravity remains more or less constant for a fortnight, the wine can be racked, sulphited and stabilised with potassium sorbate and further sweetened to taste. To obtain the best from the ingredients you have used, it should then be matured in the demijohn for 2 or 3 months before bottling it ready for consumption.

If you cannot obtain fresh rosehips, dried rosehips and rosehip 'shells' (dried outer casings) can be bought from winemaking suppliers. These should be used, as for most dried materials, at one-quarter of the rate recommended for fresh rosehips.

A way of storing the goodness of rosehips is by using them to make a rich syrup that will keep for several months if properly prepared.

ROSEHIP SYRUP

2 ¼ lb (1 kg) fully-ripened rosehips
1 lb (450 g) granulated sugar

Top and tail the hips – they may just be going slightly soft and mushy – and put them through a coarse-bladed mincer or a kitchen liquidiser.

Place the pulp in a pan with 2 pints (1.1 litres) of water, bring to the boil and simmer for 10 minutes. Strain without any pressure through a very fine cloth, or a jellybag if you have one and put the liquid extract to one side. Replace the pulp in the pan, add a further 2 pints of water and repeat the process.

When the second batch has been strained the pulp should be discarded. Mark on the outside of a large pan the level for 2 pints (1.1 litres), then pour into the pan all the liquid extract plus 1 lb (450 g) of granulated sugar. Bring to the boil, stirring to dissolve the sugar, then continue boiling until the contents of the pan are reduced to the 2 pint (1.1 litres) level.

Pour the syrup into pre-heated bottles of ½ pint (280 ml) capacity and cap to seal immediately. The bottles should be stood on an asbestos sheet or a piece of board to prevent them cracking from thermal shock. Allow them to cool slowly, then label to avoid any future confusion.

One of these bottles is sufficient to replace the grape concentrate or raisins shown as alternative ingredients in the recipes given in this book.

Fruit Juices

Once the fresh fruit harvest is over, the winemaker is then forced to rely on imported materials, or ingredients that have been preserved in some form. A constant supply of everyday white table wines can be made quickly and economically from the cartons of fruit juices commonly on sale in chain stores and supermarkets. These can be straight single-fruit extracts, or blends of several fruits, which may include such exotics as passionfruit, mango, guava and lychee. Most large firms have their own blend and it

can be quite intriguing to search them out, ferment them to a standard recipe, and compare them. The following is a typical recipe for such a wine.

BLENDED FRUIT JUICE TABLE WINE

2 pints (1 litre-pack) mixed fruit juices
1 ¾ lb (790 g) granulated sugar
1 teaspoon (5 g) nutrient
1 teaspoon (5 g) pectic enzyme
1 teaspoon (5 g) Bentonite powder
1 teaspoon (5 g) tartaric acid
1 (3 mg) Vitamin B tablet
¼ teaspoon (1.5 g) magnesium sulphate (Epsom salts)
White wine yeast
Pinch of tannin

Use a true wine yeast, to ensure the flavour remains unspoilt; one of the range of German white wine yeasts will usually prove suitable.

Convert the sugar to a syrup by boiling it in 1 pint (560 ml) of water and cooling it. Put all the ingredients except the yeast into a demijohn, top up to the shoulder of the jar with cold water and add the yeast. Fit a rubber bung and half-filled airlock and leave to ferment until dry.

Rack onto a teaspoonful (5 ml) of sulphite solution or a crushed Campden tablet, then stir in a teaspoonful (5 g) of potassium sorbate. The wine can then be sweetened if desired and bottled in the knowledge that no further fermentation will take place.

These wines are designed to be drunk while young, fresh and fruity. They do not have the alcohol or body for long maturation. It is not necessary to add any acid to orange or grapefruit juice, or any of the citrus-fruit juice blends, as they normally have a high enough citric acid content for a satisfactory fermentation.

Liqueurs

As mentioned in the introduction to this book, home distillation is both illegal and dangerous, and the only lawful way of increasing the alcohol content of your wines beyond the alcohol tolerance limit of your yeast is to add commercially produced spirits. Despite this, the blending of liqueurs at home is a popular sideline of the winemaking hobby and liqueurs can be made for a fraction of the cost of their commercial equivalents.

The distillation of fruits and herbs is far from being a modern discovery. Hippocrates commented in the fifth century BC that the ancients carried out such distillations to produce extracts suitable for use with medicines. Since the Middle Ages, distillation has been practised in Europe and this method of producing herbal extracts and digestifs led eventually to such masterpieces as Benedictine D.O.M., reputedly made from over seventy-five different herbs and plants, and the deservedly popular Drambuie, said to have originated as Bonnie Prince Charlie's personal liqueur.

Liqueurs are usually sweet and are made by combining extracts of fruits and herbs with potable spirit. This can be achieved by distilling all the ingredients together, by adding fruit or herb extracts to the spirit or, finally, by infusing the plant material in spirit so that the alcohol draws from it the required colour and flavour. This last method is the one used in making rumtopf and sloe gin.

For detailed methods of blending herbs and extracts and flavourings, and for making your own fruit extracts, you will have to refer to a specialised book on the subject. However, for most of the popular liqueurs, acceptable substitutes can be blended to suit most palates by a judicious use of bought flavourings, sugar, homemade wine and a small amount of spirit.

Flavourings similar to many of the liqueurs of commerce are available, but vary in reliability and trueness of flavour from brand to brand. Some simple flavours, such as peppermint, can be bought at any grocer's shop, but the more specialised flavourings must be obtained from winemakers' supply shops. As names such as Benedictine are registered trade marks, the flavourings cannot be given the same names, and therefore have recognisable close approximations, such as 'Dictine', or 'Green Convent' for the Chartreuse-type of liqueur. Linked with flavours are colours, and these can be achieved with the usual culinary dyes. Be careful not to use too much colouring as this can lead to some very gaudy, almost fluorescent, colours of liqueur.

The sugar used is caster, because it dissolves easily, or granulated sugar milled to a powder in a kitchen liquidiser or blender.

Wine for liqueurmaking should be sweet, as high in alcohol as possible and of a suitable colour; it should have a low or neutral taste that will be dominated by your chosen flavour or flavours, or be a wine of similar type to the finished liqueur, e.g. a citrus wine for making a Curaçao-type liqueur.

The spirit used is usually a flavourless white spirit, such as vodka, which comes in two strengths, or Polish spirit, which is also sold in two, even higher, strengths. The spirit is normally used only to increase the alcohol content of the liqueur blend, but you may wish to try substituting brandy, rum, or whisky if the added flavour will help in the finished liqueur – imitations of coffee and rum liqueur are obvious examples.

Appendix 3 gives approximate proportions of wine, sugar, syrup and spirit to blend for different types of liqueur. Liqueurs vary greatly in their alcohol content and you will find that, if you have got the balance of sweetness and taste right, it will not matter if the alcohol content is slightly below that of the commercial liqueur. The chart shows four columns for the amount of spirit to be used for various liqueur strengths and you should select the column appropriate to the spirit you are using.

By way of example, let us make up half a bottle (13 fl oz or 365 ml) of a cherry brandy-type liqueur. This is normally fairly low in alcohol, about 25% by volume, and you will need 7½ fl oz (210 ml) of sweet red wine, 2½ fl oz (70 ml) of sugar syrup and 6 fl oz (170 ml) of ordinary 37% (65° proof) vodka if that is the strength and the spirit you are using. This blend will give just over half a bottle, but you will find little difficulty in using up the excess in tasting periodically to see how the blend is progressing.

Combine the wine, sugar and spirit in a large jug, and then cautiously begin to add your flavouring. Cherry brandy tastes of the stones of the cherries and your flavour extract will probably have quite a strong almond smell, as the kernels of most stone fruits contain cyanogenetic compounds similar to those in almonds. Add the flavouring sparingly, a little at a time, stirring it really thoroughly before tasting. Clean your palate with cold water or a little dry bread before tasting again.

In addition to the commercial flavouring you have used, the liqueur's taste can be modified in other ways, such as adding a little cherry syrup, or some of the strained juice from a tin of black cherries. This is one of the joys of liqueurmaking, in that a small part of the blend can be taken and altered by adding another ingredient and tasted. If it is an improvement, a proportionately larger addition of the extra ingredient can then be blended into the bulk mixture. Many happy hours are passed like this, but do make sure you record all additions meticulously, and their proportions, so that you can repeat them later if you wish.

Although no fermentation takes place in liqueur blending, and the mixtures can be drunk at once, most of them will improve if kept for a short while in the bottle. This applies particularly to blends where several ingredients are involved, as the waiting period allows the flavours to intermingle to a greater degree than they will by simply stirring them in a jug.

To end, just two tips: firstly, a slightly harsh blend can be smoothed off by adding a little glycerine and, secondly, if you use any fresh fruit juices or extracts, remember to treat them with pectic enzyme beforehand; nothing looks worse than a hazy liqueur.

Ginger Beer

Just by way of a change, how about making a simple ginger beer? This is a popular old recipe, but like all ginger beer recipes, relies on the weak fermenting power of baker's yeast, lack of nutrient, and the fact that children and adults alike enjoy the drink. A gallon (4.5 litres) is therefore quickly consumed, before the pressure in the bottles can get too high.

GINGER BEER

1 oz (30 g) root ginger
½ oz (15 g) cream of tartar
½ oz (15 g) baker's yeast
Juice and zest of 2 lemons
1 lb (450 g) granulated sugar

Bruise the ginger with a mallet, or half-crush it with a pair of pliers, and put it into the fermenting bucket. Add all the ingredients except the yeast. Stir well to dissolve the sugar, and leave it to cool under a lid.

When the temperature has dropped to about 75°F (24°C) cream the yeast in a half-cup of the liquor and leave in a warm place for a few minutes to activate the yeast. As soon as it is working properly, stir it into the contents of the bucket, cover, and leave for 24 hours.

Strain the ginger beer into strong beer bottles and fit clip-on plastic crown tops. *Under no circumstances must you use screw-top bottles.* The drink will be ready in 2 or 3 days and should then be stored in as cool a place as possible. Homemade ginger beer should be drunk within a week as a slow fermentation will continue and build up pressure inside the bottles. If this becomes excessive the caps will blow off as a safety valve.

Ginger beer is always cloudy and this will show when it is poured. However, there will also be a sediment of yeast and this should be left behind in the bottle where possible.

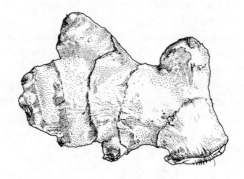

WINTER

Few British winemakers have palm trees in their gardens to tap for sap to make palm wine or toddy, but we can make wine from the fruits of two of the palm family – dates and coconuts – both of which are readily available in any grocery shop in their dried form.

Dates

Dates can be bought as fresh fruit in season, but are expensive as a winemaking ingredient compared with the dried compressed dates that are always on the shop shelves. With its rich sweet flavour, the date is an ideal material for making social or dessert wines, either on its own or combined with other fruits.

The date palm (*Phoenix dactylifera*) is an ancient tree, having been cultivated for at least the last 5000 years. It will bear fruit for anything up to 60 years, producing 100 – 150 lb (45 – 68 kg) of dates each year, so this widely grown tree of the tropics is of tremendous economic value.

Dates may contain 60% or more sugar, and this must be taken into account when using them as a winemaking ingredient.

DATE WINE

3 lb (1.4 kg) dates
2 ¼ lb (1 kg) sugar
2 teaspoons (10 g) tartaric acid
1 teaspoon (5 g) nutrient
1 teaspoon (5 g) Bentonite powder
1 teaspoon (5 g) pectic enzyme
¼ teaspoon (1.5 g) grape tannin
Wine yeast

Chop or mince the dates – extract any stones first – and place them in a bucket. Boil the sugar with 1 ½ pints (840 ml) of water and pour while still hot over the dates; add a further 4 pints (2.3 litres) of boiling water. Cover and leave to cool.

When the temperature drops to about 80°F (27°C), add the rest of the ingredients, including the yeast. Ferment on the pulp for a week, stirring daily, and then strain the must into a demijohn and fit a bung and airlock.

Rack a fortnight later and top up to the shoulder of the jar with water. Leave undisturbed until the fermentation ends, when the wine falls clear and bubbles cease to pass through the airlock. Rack onto a teaspoonful (5 ml) of sulphite solution and a ¼ teaspoonful (1.5 g) of potassium sorbate. The wine can then be sweetened if desired and bottled for a few months' maturation to be at its best.

Coconuts

Coconuts are a far less well known ingredient for wine making. These large nuts are the fruit of the palm tree, *Cocos nucifera*, and wine can be made either from the sap of the tree or the 'milk' of the green nuts. However, as neither is readily obtainable in our cool climate, try this variation on the previous recipe:

COCONUT WINE
1 lb (450 g) desiccated coconut
1 lb (450 g) dates
1 lb (450 g) rice
2 ¼ lb (1 kg) sugar

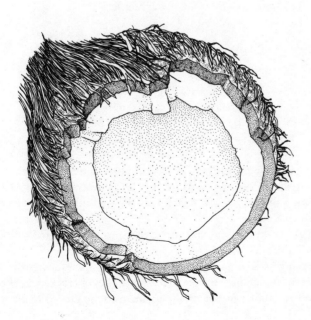

2 teaspoons (10 g) tartaric acid
1 teaspoon (5 g) nutrient
1 teaspoon (5 g) Bentonite powder
1 teaspoon (5 g) pectic enzyme
¼ teaspoon (1.5 g) grape tannin
Wine yeast

Boil the rice for 5 minutes in 1½ pints (840 ml) of water, then strain the liquid onto the dates and coconut. Simmer for 15 minutes, then strain onto the other ingredients, and continue as in the date wine recipe, adding 4 pints (2.3 litres) of boiling water and so on. This makes a surprisingly good white wine, but may need a little wine finings to clear it. If the wine happens to prove obstinately hazy, pour a small amount into a glass and add one or two drops of brown tincture of iodine. If the wine then shows a blue tinge, the haze is due to starch from the rice, and needs to be treated with an enzyme known as amylase, which, like pectic enzyme, simply needs to be stirred into the wine. However, don't be discouraged, as a starch haze is not common with this recipe.

Christmas Mull

December is a favourite time for festivities and one of the best ways of welcoming guests on a cold day or night is to make some mulled wine. This is a simple process, consisting of heating wine and other liquids if wanted with sugar and spices. This produces a drink that will quickly drive out winter's chill and replace it with a warm suffusing glow. Try some, from the following recipe.

ROY'S CHRISTMAS MULL
2 pints (1 litre) red wine
2 pints (1 litre) lemonade
¼ bottle (200 ml approx) dark rum
8 oz (225 g) sugar (boiled with ¼ pint/140 ml water)
½ teaspoon (2.5 g) each of powdered nutmeg, cinnamon, mixed spice and ginger
6 cloves
½ pint (280 ml) fruit juice (a 'tropical blend' is recommended)

Place all the ingredients, except the rum, in a large saucepan or a preserving pan. Heat gently until piping hot, then simmer for 10 – 15 minutes to blend the spices smoothly into the flavour.

Remove the pan from the heat and stir in the rum. Garnish with slices of orange and lemon, while still very hot.

If you are serving your mull from a glass punch bowl, remember to preheat the bowl with warm, and then hot, water, to prevent it being cracked by the heat of the mulled wine. When ladling or pouring the wine into the glasses to serve it, a metal

teaspoon stood in the glass will similarly reduce the chance of damage from thermal shock, and can be removed straight away.

Do not use your best wine for a mull; it is in fact an excellent way of using up any wine that you are too proud to offer your friends on its own, because of some minor imperfection or lack of quality.

The quantities and ingredients in this recipe have been arrived at by trial and error. Don't hesitate to alter quantities, or substitute other ingredients, tasting and modifying the recipe as you go along. Quite apart from the fact that alcohol would largely evaporate if simmered, this is a good reason for not adding the spirits, the most expensive ingredient, until the last moment.

Rumtopf

With the approach of Christmas, comes the time to open up the rumtopf that has been quietly maturing all Summer and Autumn. Unscrew the lid, and just take a breath of that rich infusion of rum and fresh fruit; there's nothing else that has that same heavy sweet aroma and it is worth savouring for a moment.

Some of the liquid nectar can then be carefully decanted. This may be slightly hazy, but as no other liqueur has such a blend of ingredients to titillate the palate, simply serve it in tinted or patterned glasses.

The rich compôte of fruit that remains can be eaten on its own, with cream, ice cream or custard, as a trifle ingredient, or with Christmas pudding – in fact, at any time at all. If by some strange chance some remains after the festivities, add a little fresh rum to the fruit and use it as the base to start off the New Year's rumtopf.

Carrots

One wine that can be started in December is carrot. This is one of the few root vegetables that makes a good wine, expecially if helped with a few raisins or some grape concentrate. Carrot wine can develop quite a strong spiritous flavour, especially if grain is included, and is sometimes referred to as 'carrot whisky'. The recipe that follows is for an acceptable carrot wine that does not have this flavour, which is uncharacteristic for a wine.

MEDIUM SWEET CARROT WINE

3 lb (1.4 kg) carrots
3 ¼ lb (1.5 kg) sugar
8 oz (225 g) chopped raisins (or 6 fl oz/170 ml can of white grape concentrate)
1 teaspoon (5 g) nutrient
1 ½ teaspoons (7.5 g) tartaric acid
1 teaspoon (5 g) Bentonite powder
1 (3 mg) Vitamin B tablet
Sherry yeast

Boil the sugar in 1 ¾ pints (980 ml) of water and leave to cool. Scrub, top and tail the carrots and cut into small chunks or strips. Simmer them for 15 – 20 minutes in 2 pints (1.1 litres) of unsalted water, until just tender when prodded with a fork, and then strain the liquid into the fermenting bucket. (The carrots can be dropped into boiling unsalted water afterwards to be eaten as a vegetable, or just fed to your favourite pony as a Christmas treat.) To the bucket, add the sugar syrup, raisins (or grape concentrate) and 2 ½ pints (1.4 litres) of water. The nutrient, acid, Bentonite and Vitamin B tablet should also be stirred in and the yeast added as soon as the temperature is down to 80°F (27°C). If grape concentrate has been used, the must can be transferred to a demijohn and left until the fermentation ends, or the wine

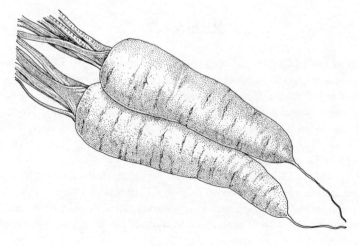

yeast reduces the sugar content to the degree of sweetness you are aiming for – about SG 1.010 – 1.015.

If raisins or any other solids are included in the recipe, the fermentation should take place in the bucket for the first week; the must is then strained into the demijohn and the fermentation allowed to continue in the same way. Stabilise the finished wine by racking it onto a teaspoonful (5 ml) of sulphite solution, or a crushed Campden tablet, and a ¼ teaspoonful (1.5 g) of potassium sorbate.

A reminder – don't salt the water which you use for simmering the carrots or you'll have salty wine, and don't overcook the carrots or the wine may have a persistent haze when finished.

An interesting variation on this recipe is to use a 6 oz (170 ml) can of red grape concentrate instead of the white concentrate suggested. This results in the gallon of wine being tinted a delightful rose pink, and makes it most unlikely that your friends will recognise the wine as being made from carrots.

Raisins

Raisins have been mentioned numerous times already as an ingredient to use to add a little vinosity, or grapiness, to wines that do not include grapes or concentrated grape juice. But of course raisins are dried grapes and, as such, will make a perfectly good wine if used as the main ingredient.

Using just raisins without added sugar is an expensive way of making wine, as 8 – 10 lb (3.6 – 4.5 kg) of fruit are needed to make a good full-bodied sweet wine. A reasonable compromise is to reduce the amount of fruit, add a little banana to help give body to the wine, and use sugar to increase the potential alcohol content.

The following recipe will give a pleasing sweet wine. If possible buy the large muscatel raisins for this wine, as their distinctive flavour is particularly suited to strong sweet wines.

RAISIN SOCIAL WINE

4 lb (1.8 kg) raisins, preferably muscatel
2 ¼ lb (1 kg) granulated sugar
1 lb (450 g) bananas
1 teaspoon (5 g) nutrient
1 teaspoon (5 g) pectic enzyme
1 teaspoon (5 g) Bentonite powder
1 (3 mg) Vitamin B tablet
Wine yeast – Sherry or Malaga

Chop or mince the raisins and peel and slice the bananas. Place both fruits in a large pan with 3 pints (1.7 litres) water and bring slowly to the boil. Simmer for 20 minutes, then pour the contents of the pan into the bucket containing the sugar. Stir well to dissolve, then add the nutrient, acid and Vitamin B tablet.

Add 3 pints (1.7 litres) of cold water and leave to cool to 80°F (27°C) then add the pectic enzyme and yeast. Ferment on the pulp for 4 or 5 days, then strain, without pressing, into a demijohn. Add the Bentonite powder and fit the rubber bung and half-filled airlock. Rack off the sediment after a fortnight, then top up to the shoulder of the jar with water. Add a further 4 oz (115 g) of sugar dissolved in a little of the must, warmed in a pan, each time the specific gravity drops to SG 1.000 or the wine tastes dry. Finally, stabilise by racking onto 1 teaspoonful (5 ml) of sulphite solution and a ¼ teaspoonful (1.5 g) of potassium sorbate. Adjust the sweetness to taste and store to mature in bulk for a month or so. Remember, if you use an airlock during this period, to check periodically that the airlock has not dried out. Keep it topped up; a little glycerine in the water will slow the rate of evaporation. If a solid bung is used, make sure that it is cork, not rubber, as a rubber bung will slowly perish and adhere to the neck of the demijohn and become difficult to remove. A cork bung will also allow a small amount of oxygen to seep into the demijohn, which helps the wine to mature and develop.

After Christmas and New Year, you will find your wine stocks will have shrunk alarmingly. This is a good time to try out some of the many commercial wine kits and cans that are on the market, as generally speaking they ferment out in a few weeks and can be used for rapid replenishment of your cellar.

Whether you are buying wine kits or beer kits, what you get depends largely on what you are prepared to pay. Many of the cheaper kits have the grape concentrate or the malt extended by the inclusion of sugar or glucose syrup, and thus are not the bargains that they first appear to be. All wrappers or packages state the contents in descending order of quantity of each ingredient, so it is easy to see whether you are paying for the water in a glucose syrup at grape-juice-concentrate prices, or buying sugar at the same cost as expensive malt extract. Seemingly expensive kits often prove to be the better bargains.

Tangerines, Mandarins and Satsumas

Favourite, almost traditional, fruits for the Christmas period are oranges and their smaller relatives, the tangerines, mandarins, and satsumas. Immediately after the holidays, these fruits are at their cheapest and the smaller varieties in particular make a light and delicate white wine.

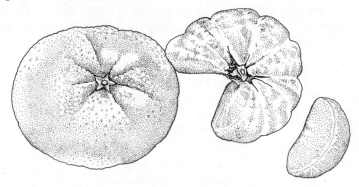

WHITE TABLE TANGERINE WINE

15-20 tangerines, mandarins or satsumas, according to size

2 ¼ lb (1 kg) sugar

1 teaspoon (5 g) nutrient

1 teaspoon (5 g) pectin enzyme

8 oz (225 g) minced sultanas (or 6 fl oz/170 ml white grape concentrate)

White wine yeast

Extract the juice from the fruit. Add the sugar as a cooled syrup, plus 5 pints (2.8 litres) of cold water and the remainder of ingredients, and stir well. Add the yeast and cover. Stir daily for 5 days, then strain into a demijohn. Top up to the shoulder of the jar with cold water and fit a bung and airlock. Leave to ferment until dry and rack onto a teaspoonful (5 ml) of sulphite solution. If you prefer to sweeten this wine slightly, add a ¼ teaspoonful (1.5 g) of potassium sorbate as well as the sulphite solution. This wine can be bottled and should be drunk while still young. It will not improve with long maturation and should be drunk within 12 months of the fermentation commencing.

Tea

There are few ingredients that are inexpensive, available all the year round and readily on sale at every grocers' shop. One notable exception is tea; tea wine costs little to make and can be started off at any time or season as long as there is a warm enough spot, or artificial heating, to sustain yeast activity.

Many old recipes advise the would-be winemaker to save the tea remaining in the pot until sufficient has been accumulated to make a gallon of wine. Perhaps this was necessary 40 years or so ago, when tea was rationed in the United Kingdom, but saving odd quantities of well-stewed cold tea is certainly not to be recommended. As the following recipe shows, the amount of tea used is insignificant and freshly made tea is markedly superior in every way for winemaking, just as it is for drinking as tea. There are numerous different teas on sale and these will make wines that differ slightly, the scented Earl Grey is a good example of this variation. Loose packet tea is preferable to tea-bags for our purposes.

TEA WINE

6 pints (3.4 litres) hot, fresh tea, strained
2¼ lb (1 kg) sugar
8 oz (225 g) chopped raisins
Juice and zest of 2 lemons
1 teaspoon (5 g) nutrient
1 teaspoon (5 g) pectic enzyme
Wine yeast

Pour the strained hot tea over the sugar and stir well to dissolve. Add the raisins, lemon juice and zest and nutrient. Cover and allow to cool, then add the pectic enzyme and wine yeast. Cover and ferment for 5 days, stirring daily.

Strain the must into a demijohn and leave for the fermentation to reach conclusion. Rack onto a teaspoonful (5 ml) each of sulphite solution and potassium sorbate and sweeten slightly. Because of its tannin content, this wine will keep well, but can be drunk while still young if the need arises.

Mulled Ale

January and February are usually the coldest months of the year and a tankard of mulled ale will quickly warm you through. Mulled ale is simply beer, usually a nice brown ale or mild beer, heated in a pan with a couple of teaspoonfuls (10 ml) of brown sugar, a pinch of powdered nutmeg and ginger, and perhaps a clove. Don't boil the mixture, just heat it up thoroughly, then pour it into a pewter mug or pre-heated glass. Sit in your favourite chair and sip this, and you will soon be glowing from head to toe. And you will have little difficulty in going to sleep if you take a glass piping hot as a nightcap.

Seville Oranges

February sees the Seville orange on sale for marmalade-making, and excellent marmalade it makes too, alone or mixed with other citrus fruits. But it will also make good aperitif wines, so buy a few pounds extra and make up a gallon from the recipe below. The bitterness of Seville orange wine fades a little with storage, but the wine remains fresh and tangy, just right to clean your palate and sharpen your appetite before a meal.

You can make this wine at other times of the year by substituting for the fresh Seville oranges one of the tins of prepared oranges sold for making marmalade.

SEVILLE ORANGE APERITIF

10-12 Seville oranges
3 lb (1.4 kg) sugar
½ pint (280 ml) white grape concentrate (or 12 oz/340 g minced sultanas)
1 teaspoon (5 g) nutrient
1 teaspoon (5 g) Bentonite powder
2 teaspoons (10 g) pectic enzyme
1 (3 mg) Vitamin B tablet
½ teaspoon (1.5 g) tannin
Wine yeast

Extract the juice from the oranges and put in the bucket with the zest of the peel. Boil the sugar in 1½ pints (840 ml) of water and pour it into the bucket while hot. Add the other ingredients, except the pectic enzyme and yeast, plus 4 pints (2.3 litres) of cold water. Check the temperature, and put in the enzyme and yeast when it has dropped to 80°F (27°C) or less.

Ferment on the pulp for 6 days, stirring daily, then strain through a cloth into a sterilised demijohn. Fit a bung and airlock, and leave to ferment to dry and clear. Rack onto a teaspoonful (5 ml) of sulphite solution or a crushed Campden tablet, and stabilise with a teaspoonful (5 g) of potassium sorbate. The wine can then be sweetened slightly – very sweet aperitifs do not stimulate the appetite as they should do – and mature for a month or longer before bottling the wine to drink it. This wine can be varied by using say, six Seville oranges and six sweet oranges, to get a less bitter wine that can be drunk sooner.

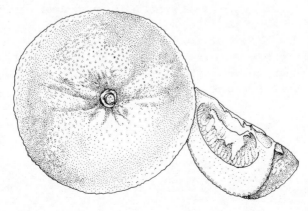

Grapefruit

Grapefruit are in season now, and grapefruit wine can be made in the same way as the tangerine or Seville orange wines. Grapefruit make a good aperitif, but as with all citrus fruits, the white pith is excessively bitter and should not be used; restrict your ingredients to just the juice and the zest, which contains volatile oils that help to give your wine its tangy fruit flavour. In addition to their bitterness, the pith, pulp and pips all contain large amounts of pectin, another good reason for excluding them from your wine.

Parsnips

Following winter's frosts, parsnips are now at their sweetest and will make an excellent wine. The method and the ingredients are just the same as for the carrot wine on page 130, and a good wine is practically guaranteed. Parsnip wine has often been likened to sherry and this can be made more apparent by using a sherry yeast and maturing the finished wine for 3 or 4 months with a bung of compressed cotton wool replacing the usual solid cork bung or bored rubber bung and airlock. This wine is also improved if 8 oz (225 g) of soft brown sugar is substituted for an equal quantity of the white sugar in the recipe.

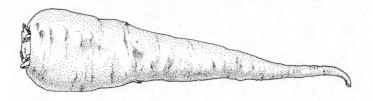

Exotic Fruits

Winter wines can be made from all sorts of canned and frozen fruits and the range available gives the home winemaker the opportunity of making wine from a great variety of truly exotic ingredients. Any supermarket will sell at least some of the following and all of them should be available to the winemaker who is willing to ask at chainstores, local grocers, delicatessens and health food stores: tinned mango, pawpaw, lychee (or litchi), loganberries, guavas and apricots; bottled maple syrup, and passion fruit juice; kumquats, fresh uglis, passion fruit, kiwi fruit (also known as Chinese gooseberries), prickly pears (*Opuntia* cactus fruit), persimmons and cranberries.

This is not an exhaustive list and a keen and acquisitive winemaker will undoubtedly be able to add to it with a little perserverance. Ethnic supply shops, catering for a minority group, will often produce unexpected materials, such as the rambutans the author obtained from a Chinese shop.

As an example of a wine from an exotic fruit, try this recipe for a light dry wine.

WHITE TABLE LYCHEE WINE

2 × 11 oz (310 g) cans lychees (or 2 lb/900 g fresh lychees)
2 ¼ lb (1 kg) granulated white sugar
1 teaspoon (5 g) nutrient
1 teaspoon (5 g) citric acid
1 teaspoon (5 g) pectic enzyme
1 teaspoon (5 g) Bentonite powder
White wine yeast

Tip the contents of the two cans into a sterilised bucket and crush the fruit with a potato-masher. If using fresh lychees, flake off the brittle skin, remove the large stones unbroken and crush the remaining pulp. Shelling and stoning the fruit should be done over the bucket to prevent the loss of precious juice.

Boil the sugar in 1 ¼ pints (700 ml) of water, cool the resulting syrup and add it to the bucket. Pour in a further 5 pints (2.8 litres) of cold water; the other ingredients and the yeast can now be added. Note that, although neither skin nor stalks are included in this recipe, no tannin need be added to the pulped lychees.

Ferment in the bucket for 5 or 6 days, then strain into a demijohn. Leave the wine to ferment to dry, then rack onto a teaspoonful (5 ml) of sulphite solution. If

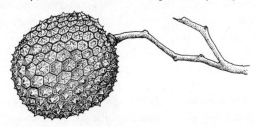

the wine needs sweetening slightly, either use a non-fermenting sweetener or add a teaspoonful (5 g) of potassium sorbate and a little sugar syrup.

This can be used as a basic recipe for almost any material for which you do not have a recipe. For some white wine ingredients, it may be necessary to add a little tannin, say ¼ teaspoonful (1.5 g), and the amount of acid can vary from none to 2 teaspoonfuls (10 g) depending on how acid, or tart, the flavour of the main ingredient. To be sure on this point, it is best to make up a a gallon (4.5 litres) of must and test the acidity, either with a simple test-paper strip or, more accurately, by following the method of titration described in Appendix 1. When you have tried a new ingredient and find you like it as a wine, then later batches can be improved by adding ½ pint (280 ml) of grape concentrate, or raisins, bottled grape juice or a fresh fruit, to vary the flavour or bouquet and to add body and vinosity if needed. The permutations are almost infinite. Will you be telling the winemaking world of your superb new recipe? A lot of winemakers are looking for an original recipe they can copy; why shouldn't it be yours?

Stout

And now Winter is coming to an end and the first signs of Spring are giving advance warning of another year. There will be a lot to do in the garden, so prepare for the chilly days and busy hours with a strong and warming stout from this recipe for 1 gallon.

DRY IRISH-TYPE STOUT

2 oz (60 g) crushed roast barley
1 lb (450 g) dark dried malt extract
1 ½ oz (45 g) Fuggles hops
2 oz (60 g) crushed crystal malt
Beer yeast – top-fermenting
1 ½ oz (45 g) granulated white sugar

Place the crushed roasted barley, malt extract, hops and crystal malt in a large pan with 4 pints (2.3 litres) of water and bring to the boil slowly. Keep stirring to ensure the malt extract dissolves and does not stick to the pan and burn. Simmer this wort for about 20 minutes, stirring occasionally, then strain into a bucket through a nylon bag or a piece of muslin or similar cloth fastened round the bucket rim with clothes pegs.

Sprinkle a kettleful of hot water over the spent hops and malt husks to wash out the sweet wort trapped there – i.e. sparge the strainings – and remove the hops and husks to add to your compost heap. Cover the bucket and leave to stand until the contents cool.

When the temperature has dropped to 80°F (27°C), pitch the yeast and replace the cover. The wort should be fermenting well within a day and after 2, or perhaps 3 days there will be a thick foam on the surface, comprising froth stiffened with surplus yeast. Skim this off and, with a clean, damp sulphited cloth, wipe away any ring of dark brown gummy substance at surface level on the side of the bucket. This is made up of excessively harsh hop resins and yeast and needs to be removed to prevent it spoiling the flavour of the beer.

Keep the wort covered until the fermentation has ended, when just a few bubbles will be rising centrally and the top ½ inch (13 mm) of surface beer will be clearing visibly. Stir in a little beer finings at this stage and the stout should be ready to rack off the sediment 24 – 36 hours later.

Dissolve the white sugar in ½ pint (280 ml) of hot water and stir it into the freshly racked stout. The sugar will condition the stout, i.e. it will cause it to ferment in the bottles. This is because it activates the traces of yeast that remain and carbon dioxide gas is produced which makes the stout sparkling and lively, producing the fine bubbles that make up the head on the stout.

To make this a sweet stout, add 4 oz (115 g) lactose, which is a non-fermenting sweetener, and reduce the hops to 1 oz (30 g).

Bottle the stout, after topping it up with water to a full gallon (4.5 litres) if necessary. Use only bottles made up to take repeated pressure, such as the returnable ones used for beer, sparkling cider or lemonade. Keep in a warm place for 3 or 4 days to condition, then store in the cool for another 2 weeks or so to mature.

When you pour any homebrewed beer, remember to pour it all in one continuous movement, so the yeast sediment does not get disturbed until almost all the beer has been poured. Ensure that you have two glasses, or a pint mug or a large jug to hold all the beer and a bit of froth. The beer is now ready for you to enjoy.

If you have difficulty obtaining roasted barley, buy plain barley and cook it in a roasting tin in the oven until brown.

By the way, you have now made stout, matured it, poured it and enjoyed drinking it. Have you thought about the bottles and glasses? The bottles should be rinsed with clean cold water to remove any sediment and then stored with a few drops of diluted sulphite solution to keep them sweet until refilled with your next brew. The glasses should be washed in clean hot water, free from any soap or detergent, and dried while hot with a clean glasscloth that was well rinsed in fresh water before being dried. Unless you use the trade cleaning agents, you run a great risk of detergent soaps leaving a trace on your glass or glasscloth which will ruin the head on your beer when it has been poured. This applies also to the finishing agent put in dishwashing machines to give the dishes and glasses a gleaming finish. Unfortunately, all these materials operate by breaking down surface tension, and this effectively ruins the head on the beer by destroying the bubbles as fast as they are produced. Clean hot water takes a lot of beating!

Sparkling Wines

The last beverage in this volume is the finest, the most enjoyable, and the most complex – in fact, a type of wine that needs all the skill, care and attention you can give it. Your efforts will be well rewarded with wines that will impress those who taste them and justifiably fill you with pride.

Sparkling wines produced commercially are always more expensive in the United Kingdom than still wines of comparable quality. This is because they are taxed at a higher rate of duty, as luxuries, because heavier stronger bottles and special corks are required, and the labour costs for their production, particularly those made by the champagne method, are higher than for other wines. But there is no reason why a homewinemaker should not make his or her own sparkling wines. The process is virtually the same as making bottled beer with good sparkling condition, i.e. the basic must is fermented out to dryness and then re-fermented in the bottle with a little extra sugar. Where sparkling wines differ from bottled beers is that the yeast from the bottle fermentation of wine is usually disgorged from the bottle before the wine is ready to drink.

Red wines can have a sparkle – the Italian Lambrusco is an example of this – but such wines are not common. Rosé wines may have a slight prickle from the carbon dioxide gas dissolved in them, with Mateus Rosé being the best known wine of this type. Wines of these two types are not fully effervescent and are described either as *pétillant* (French) or *spritzig* (German), and can occur in amateur wines that are bottled without proper sulphiting and dosing with potassium sorbate. Such re-fermentations can arise from stray yeast cells acting on a little residual sugar in the wine, or by bacterial action by a lactobacillus that converts malic acid to lactic acid, releasing a little carbon dioxide as it does so. These two types of activity in bottled wines gave rise to the old belief that wines would 'work' again in the Spring, with the flowering of the parent apple, gooseberry, or whatever. The renewed activity follows simply from instability in the wine and the seasonal increase in temperature.

This book does not set out to describe in detail the various processes of commercial champagne production; the amateur process almost exactly parallels the *méthode champenoise* by which all champagnes are made, as indeed are the many equivalent wines from other countries that must call their wines by another name. The use of the term 'champagne' is restricted by law to the French wines made in the restricted area surrounding Rheims and Epernay by this method only.

To make a sparkling wine by the *méthode champenoise* at home is not particularly difficult, but for safety's sake care is needed at various stages and attention is drawn to these points as they arise.

Any light white wine with less than 12% alcohol can be converted into a sparkling wine provided that no sulphite, potassium sorbate, or other sterilising or stabilising agent has been added after the fermentation in the demijohn. Apple, gooseberry and rhubarb are probably the commonest ingredients, but this may be partly because they are easily and cheaply obtained. Grapes, grape concentrates, peaches, pears and other white-juice fruits are equally acceptable, either singly or blended. If you do not have a suitable dry wine available, then you can make up a grape-juice-concentrate kit for a gallon (4.5 litres) of medium or dry wine, and refrain from using any of the chemicals supplied for use after the fermenting period has ended, except for clearing or fining materials such as Bentonite, gelatine or isinglass. When the fermentation in the demijohn has ended, add an active champagne yeast culture and continue from Step 2 below. Alternatively you can make a basic wine as follows:

SPARKLING APPLE WINE

4 lb (1.8 kg) crushed apples
1 lb (450 g) sultanas
1 lb (450 g) granulated sugar
1 teaspoon (5 g) nutrient
1 teaspoon (5 g) Bentonite powder
1 teaspoon (5 g) tartaric acid
1 teaspoon (5 g) pectic enzyme
Champagne or Perlschaum yeast culture

Step 1 Crush the apples and cover with a teaspoonful (5 ml) of sulphite solution in 2 pints (1.1 litres) of cold water. Mince the sultanas and put them into the bucket, or pour in the grape concentrate, and add the pectic enzyme (err on the generous side with this). Cover and leave for 24 hours. Boil the sugar in ½ pint (280 ml) of water and leave to cool.

Next day add the sugar syrup, 5 pints (2.8 litres) of water and all other ingredients, including the yeast. Ferment on the pulp for 5 days, stirring daily, then strain, without pressing the pulp, into a demijohn. Fit a bored rubber bung and half-filled airlock and leave to ferment out to complete dryness.

Step 2 When the fermentation has ended, rack the wine off the sediment and check the specific gravity with a hydrometer. To be sure of an accurate reading, draw off sufficient wine for your test jar and shake it well in a bottle. This will get rid of the dissolved carbon dioxide that would otherwise buoy up the hydrometer and give a false reading.

The specific gravity should be 0.995 or less. If it has reached this level, the wine should be primed with 2½ oz (75 g) of sugar dissolved in a little of the wine warmed in a small saucepan, or 3 fl oz (85 ml) of standard sugar syrup can be stirred in thoroughly. The wine can then be bottled as described below.

If the specific gravity exceeds 0.995, then the sugar content of the wine should be checked with a Clinitest kit, obtainable from any chemist. (The Clinitest is made for checking the urine sugar content of people suffering from sugar diabetes, but the instructions work perfectly well if applied to wine, and given an accurate measurement of invert sugar in solution. There should not be any sucrose still in the wine at this stage.)

If the Clinitest shows more than 1½% sugar then the wine must either be

141

fermented further or diluted with water. At 1½ % sugar the wine is ready for bottling. Add ½ oz (15 g) for each ¼ % below 1 ½ %, thus:

% Clinitest	Sugar to add
1 ½	0
1 ¼	½ oz (15 g)
1	1 oz (30 g)
¾	1 ½ oz (45 g)
½	2 oz (60 g)
¼ -0	2 ½ oz (75 g)

Thus a wine with 1 % residual sugar, according to the Clinitest, needs 1 oz (30 g) of sugar dissolved in it to reach the correct level of 2 ½ oz (75 g) per gallon (4.5 litres).

After adjusting the sugar content of the wine, it should be syphoned into the correct type of sparkling wine bottles. These are heavier and of thicker glass than still wine bottles, and therefore have slightly larger outside measurements. Discard any bottles with chips, scratches, or any other flaws or damage, as they will need to take up to 60 lb per square inch (4.2 kg per cm^2) pressure from the wine fermentation gases.

Use hollow plastic stoppers to seal the bottles, fastening them in place with muselets (wire cages) that prevent them blowing out. A simple double loop can be made from galvanised wire (see Appendix 4) and, if these are used, a small coin or metal washer should be placed on the top of the stopper to prevent the wire cutting through the plastic.

Store the bottles in a warm room for about a week, then place them upside down in a crate, giving them a quarter-turn sharply backwards and forwards each day until all the yeast has settled in or by the hollow stoppers. Prepare a bucket of mixed ice and salt for a freezing mixture and push the bottle necks down into this. The wine and yeast in the bottle necks should soon freeze and you can then remove the muselet, the stopper and the frozen or slushy yeast deposit with very little loss of wine or effervescence. The bottles should be topped up with brandy or wine, and a non-fermenting sweetener if a sweeter wine is desired. The bottles may then be fitted with a clean stopper and muselet and stored horizontally until you wish to sample one. The chosen bottle should be chilled not frozen; about half an hour in the door-rack of a domestic refrigerator should be enough.

Once the wine has been put into champagne bottles, it should thereafter always be handled with a towel wrapped round it. Even commercial producers lose some of their bottles and with any sparkling wine there is a slight possibility of a bottle bursting. Stoppers should be eased out by twisting them, rather than letting them fly off like a bullet – think of that tremendous pressure behind them. The pressure exerted by commercial sparkling wines ranges from 75 – 90 lb per square inch (5.3 – 6.3 kg per cm^2) but this is more than an amateur should expect when using secondhand bottles.

There is now more than one kind of patent stopper on the market designed to prevent excessive pressure building up and to dispense with the need to disgorge the yeast sediment. Your winemaking supply shop should stock at least one of them that you can try if you wish.

Wine can also be given a sparkle by artificial means. One way is to chill the wine, then charge it with carbon dioxide gas, using one of the popular machines sold for making fizzy drinks at home. Another method is to fill a Sparklets soda-syphon with chilled wine instead of water, charge it with gas from a bulb in the usual way, and shake it well so the wine takes up some of the gas. The syphon is then inverted and the trigger released to vent off the surplus gas. After the syphon is turned the right way up, the cap and internal fittings removed, and the wine poured as if from a decanter.

Both of these methods will put a temporary fizz in the wine, on a par with carbonated soft drinks like lemonade. Sparkling wine that has undergone bottle refermentation and maturing actually absorbs the gas into the liquid and it is slowly released over a longer period as a fine head (strings of bubbles). This is one of the indications of a true champagne-type wine, a wine of which you should be proud and a demonstration of your skill as a winemaker.

APPENDIX 1: Acidity Measurement (Titration)

This method of measuring the acid content of a must relies on two chemicals, phenolphthalein, which is a laxative, and sodium hydroxide, which is a highly corrosive caustic. Care is therefore essential in the handling of these materials, particularly the sodium hydroxide, and in their secure storage away from children when not in use. Should any of the caustic solution be spilled, it should be copiously irrigated with fresh water, especially if splashed on the skin.

REQUIREMENTS

Wine or must for testing
Distilled water
1% phenolphthalein solution
N10 (decinormal) sodium hydroxide solution
Large test-tube or small flask
2 plastic syringes, graduated in millilitres (hypodermic needles not required)

Using one syringe, place 10 ml of must in the test-tube. Add 100 ml of water and 2 or 3 drops of phenolphthalein. Shake well to mix.

Now part-fill the other syringe with caustic soda (sodium hydroxide), noting the reading to which it is filled. Let a few drops fall into the test-tube and you will find the solution turns pink. This colour will fade as the test-tube is again shaken. Repeat this process, adding sodium hydroxide a drop at a time until a stable colour is produced which does not fade when shaken.

At this point, read off from the syringe the amount of sodium hydroxide used. From this and the following table, you can ascertain the number of parts per thousand of acid in terms of either tartaric acid or sulphuric acid; the latter, though not used as an ingredient in winemaking, was for many years used as a standard for measuring acids in wine. Fractional parts per thousand (ppt) have been rounded.

As the acid content of a must increases slightly during fermentation, you should aim at a must acidity (as tartaric acid) of 4 – 5 parts per thousand for dry wines, increasing to 5 – 6 parts per thousand for sweet wines.

A level teaspoonful (5g) of tartaric acid will increase acidity by just over 1 part per thousand. Reduction of acidity should be made by dilution of the must before fermentation, adding low-acid fruits, such as banana, to compensate for lack of body if necessary. Alternatively, a level teaspoonful (5g) of sodium bicarbonate or precipitated chalk will reduce the acidity of a gallon (4.5 litres) of must by 1 part per thousand.

Sodium hydroxide mls used	Tartaric acid p.p.t.	Sulphuric acid p.p.t.
0.5	0.4	0.25
1	0.8	0.5
2	1.5	1
3	2.25	1.5
4	3	2
5	3.75	2.5
6	4.5	3
7	5.25	3.5
8	6	4
9	6.75	4.5
10	7.5	5

APPENDIX 2: Gravity Readings, Sugar Content and Potential Alcohol

Specific gravity	Sugar content per gallon (4.5 litres) oz (g)	% potential alcohol by volume
1.000	0 (0)	0
1.005	3 (85)	1
1.010	5 (140)	1 ½
1.015	7 (200)	2 ½
1.020	9 (225)	3 ½
1.025	12 (340)	4 ½
1.030	13 (370)	5
1.035	16 (450)	6
1.040	17 (480)	6 ½
1.045	20 (570)	7 ½
1.050	22 (620)	8
1.055	24 (680)	9
1.060	26 (740)	9 ½
1.065	28 (790)	10 ½
1.070	30 (850)	11 ½
1.075	32 (900)	12
1.080	34 (960)	13
1.085	36 (1020)	13 ½
1.090	39 (1100)	14 ½
1.095	41 (1160)	15
1.100	43 (1220)	16
1.105	45 (1280)	16 ½
1.110	47 (1330)	17 ½
1.115	50 (1420)	18 ½
1.120	51 (1450)	19
1.125	53 (1500)	20
1.130	56 (1590)	21
1.135	58 (1640)	21 ½
1.140	60 (1700)	22
1.145	62 (1760)	23
1.150	64 (1800)	24
1.155	66 (1900)	24 ½
1.160	68 (1930)	25 ½

APPENDIX 3: Blending Your Own Liqueurs

TO MAKE ONE HALF-BOTTLE OF LIQUEUR BY BLENDING

Liqueur strength (%) *or (Degrees proof)	Sweet wine	Sugar syrup	Polish Spirit		Vodka	
			80% (140°)	57% (100°)	45.8% (80°)	37% (65°)
	fl.oz. (ml)	fl.oz. (ml)	fl.oz.(ml)	fl.oz.(ml)	fl.oz.(ml)	fl.oz.(ml)
43% (75°)	4½ (126)	2½ (70)	6 (168)	8½ (238)	10½ (297)	–
40% (70°)	5 (140)	2½ (70)	5½ (154)	7 (196)	8½ (238)	–
32% (55°)	6½ (182)	2½ (70)	4 (112)	5½ (154)	7 (196)	8½ (238)
26% (45°)	7½ (210)	2½ (70)	3 (84)	4 (112)	5 (140)	6½ (182)
Examples: Cherry brandy 25% (43°)	7½ (210)	2½ (70)	3 (84)	4 (112)	5 (140)	6 (168)
Cointreau 40% (70°)	5 (140)	2½ (70)	5½ (154)	7 (196)	8½ (238)	–

Average wine strength 12 – 13%   Sugar syrup: 2 lb in 1 pint water
(° – °)   (900 g in 560 ml water)

Usual liqueur strengths:
   Apricot Brandy 25% to 40% (43° to 70°)   Grand Marnier 39% 68°
   Benedictine 42% (73°)   Maraschino 32% (55°)
   Cointreau 40% (70°)   Strega 43% (75°)
   Crème de Menthe 30% (52°)   Tia Maria 32% (55°)
   Curaçao 30% to 40% (52° to 70°)   Yellow Chartreuse 43% (75°)
   Drambuie 40% (70°)

Note 1: This table was compiled using 80% Polish spirit. If you use the other strengths of spirit the amount needed is greater. The amount of wine should be reduced by a corresponding amount, or you will have just over half-bottle. This does allow extra for sampling, but slightly reduces the strength of the liqueur.

*Note 2: Degrees proof° is an obsolete method of declaring alcohol content, but still appears on some bottle labels. It has therefore been included in case it is required for reference. Percentage alcohol by volume (%) has replaced degrees proof.

APPENDIX 4: How To Wire Sparkling Wine Stoppers

Take approximately 18 inches (45 cm) of galvanised wire and join the ends to make a loop. Twist into a figure of eight with one loop slightly larger than the other; twist two or three times.

Place the larger loop over the bottle neck, pull it tight and twist it to lock it into place round the neck of the bottle.

Pull the larger loop until it is long and narrow and then take it over the top of the stopper; twist it together with the other loop to pull the wire tight and lock the stopper into place.

APPENDIX 5: Poisonous or Unsuitable Plants for Winemaking

The toxicity of plant material varies with the strain of the particular growth, the soil and the season, the quantity used and the degree of dilution, whether fresh or dried, and numerous other factors, not least important being the susceptibility of the person ingesting the material.

It is outside the scope of this book to list every possible ingredient that could possibly be tried by a winemaker, as some people believe that anything vegetable can be turned into wine. This of course is not the case.

The following pointers and the subsequent list of plants should give a guide to the commoner plant material that should be avoided; if in doubt, then refer to a reputable reference book on this subject. Note particularly that the listing of plants in a herbal, especially the older works, such as those of Culpeper and Gerrard, does not mean that the material is safe for use by an amateur. Herbals include many plants that are harvested purely for their organic drug content. Many such plants are poisonous.

As a general rule, exclude fungi from your experiments. Many fungi need expert identification and a fungus that is classed as edible may only be so after extended cooking. Making it into wine might well have a dangerously different result. Dissolving the same materials in alcohol is not the same as cooking them. A perfect example is the ink cap *(Coprinus atramentarius)* which is usually only poisonous in the presence of alcohol. This still applies if any alcohol is drunk while the substance is still in the body and the symptoms will reappear some hours after the fungus has been eaten.

Quite apart from the dangers of using fungi, these plants are not a good basis for making up a wine must on their own, and a 'mushroom wine' or similar is really only a novelty, and not to be recommended.

The cabbage family (the Cruciferae, such as cauliflowers, Brussels sprouts and kale) contain organic compounds that lead to poor flavours and unpleasant aromas. The only exception is the wallflower, which blossom can be used for making a flower wine. Radishes, horseradish and the green tops of root vegetables, such as turnips and mangolds, are similarly unsuitable.

Avoid any plant whose name includes the word 'bane', such as baneberry, henbane and wolfsbane. 'Bane' signifies poison.

There are many plants classed as umbellifers, with long stems, often hollow, and crowns of white, cream or yellow flowers. Quite commonly, they are dismissed as cow parsley or hogweed, but in fact this group includes the ancestors of our carrot and parsnip, and several unpleasantly – even lethally – poisonous plants such as hemlock, fool's parsley and water dropworts. For safety's sake ignore all this group, with the possible exception of sweet cicely *(Myrrhis odorata)*. Its name means 'smelling of myrrh' and it is distinguished by its fragrant aniseed-like smell. It grows in Wales and the north of England and is locally common by the roadsides in the Yorkshire Dales.

LIST OF POISONOUS OR OTHERWISE UNSUITABLE PLANTS FOR WINEMAKING.

COMMON NAME	SCIENTIFIC NAME
Aconite, Winter	*Aconitum* spp.
Anemones, Pasque Flowers	*Anemone* spp.
Arum lilies (Cuckoo-Pint, Lords-and-Ladies)	*Arum maculatum*
Azaleas	*Azalea* spp.
Bryony, Black	*Tamus communis*
Bryony, White	*Bryonia dioica*
Buckthorn, Alder	*Frangula alnus*
Buckthorn, Common or Purging	*Rhamnus catharticus*
Bulbs generally (Lilies, Daffodils, Snowdrops etc)	*Lilium, Narcissus, Ornithogallum* etc
Buttercups, Marsh Marigolds, Celandine	*Ranunculus* spp.
Columbine	*Aquilegia vulgaris*
Clematis, Garden Varieties	*Clematis* spp.
Clematis, Wild (Traveller's Joy)	*Clematis vitalba*
Elder, Dwarf	*Sambucus ebulus*
Ferns, various	Pteridophyta
Foxglove	*Digitalis purpurea*
Geraniums, Cranesbills, Pelargoniums	*Geranium* spp.
Groundsel, Ragwort, Fleawort etc	*Senecio* spp.
Hellebores, Christmas Rose	*Helleborus* spp.
Hemlock	*Conium maculatum*
Honeysuckle (Woodbine) berries	*Lonicera periclymenum*
Irises (flags)	*Iris* spp.
Ivy	*Hedera helix*
Laburnum	*Laburnum anagyroides*
Laurel, Cherry	*Prunus laurocerasus*
Laurel, Portuguese	*Prunus lusitanica*
Lilac	*Syringa vulgaris*
Lobelia	*Lobelia* spp.
Lupins, various	*Lupinus* spp.
Meadow Rue, Common	*Thalictrum flavum*
Meadow Saffron	*Colchicum autumnale*
Mercury, Annual	*Mercurialis annua*
Mercury, Dog's	*Mercuralis perennis*
Mistletoe	*Viscum album*
Monkshood	*Aconitum napellus*
Nightshade, Black or Garden	*Solanum nigrum*
Nightshade, Deadly	*Atropa belladonna*
Nightshade, Woody (Bittersweet)	*Solanum dulcamara*
Paeony	*Paeonia mascula*

Poppies, various	*Papaver* spp., *Glaucium flavum*
Potatoes (ungreened tubers only are safe)	*Solanum tuberosum*
Privet, Garden, Hedge or Oval-Leaved	*Ligustrum ovalifolium*
Privet, Wild	*Ligustrum vulgare*
Rhododendron	*Rhododendron ponticum* etc
Rhubarb (sticks only are safe)	*Rheum rhaponticum*
Soapwort	*Saponaria officinalis*
Spindle-tree	*Euonymus eropaeus*
Pea, Broad-Leaved Everlasting	*Lathyrus sylvestris*
Pea, Sweet	*Lathyrus odoratus*
*Thorn-Apple (Jimson Weed)	*Datura stramonium*
Tomato (fruit only is safe)	*Lycopersicon esculentum*
Yew	*Taxus baccata*
Yew, Irish	*Taxus fastigiata*

*In the USA, 'Thorn-Apple' may refer to the fruit of the hawthorn (*Crataegus* spp.) which is harmless.

Further Reading

Home Beer and Wine Making
Berry, C.J.J. (1983) *First Steps in Winemaking.* Revised edition. Amateur
   Winemaker
Duncan, P. & Acton, B. (1967) *Progressive Winemaking.* Amateur Winemaker
Fowles, Professor G. (1982) *Must.* Gervin Press, Reading.
Line, D. (1974) *The Big Book of Brewing.* Amateur Winemaker
Parrack, A. (1978) *Commonsense Winemaking.* Amateur Winemaker
Pritchard, B. (1983) *All About Beer and Homebrewing.* Amateur Winemaker

Commercial Wines and Beers
Corran, H.S. (1975) *A History of Brewing.* David & Charles, Newton Abbot
Monckton, H.A. (1966) *A History of English Ale and Beer.* Bodley Head, London
Price, P.V. (1982) *Enjoying Wine – A Taster's Companion.* Heinemann, London
Robinson, J. (1979) *The Wine Book.* A. & C. Black (Publishers) Ltd, London.

Periodicals
Winemaker & Home Brewer Monthly. Argus Publications Ltd, Hemel Hempstead
Practical Winemaking and Brewing. Bi-monthly. Mountsorrel, Leicestershire
Wine For All Seasons. Subscription only. Gervin Press, 61 Church Road, Woodley,
   Reading, Berkshire.

Index